LIBRARIANS AND PUBLISHERS IN THE SCHOLARLY INFORMATION PROCESS:
Transition in the Electronic Age

Sponsored by the

Council on Library Resources
and the
Professional/Scholarly Publishing Division
of the
Association of American Publishers, Inc.

Report Prepared by
Linda Scovill

COUNCIL ON
LIBRARY
RESOURCES

aap
Association of American Publishers, Inc.

ISBN: 0-933636-30-X

Council on Library Resources
1400 16th Street, N.W., Suite 510
Washington, D.C. 20036-2217

The Council on Library Resources is a private operating foundation that has been a leader since 1956 in solving problems in information availability. The Council's mission extends to all types of libraries and information services. As an operating foundation, the Council performs projects and awards grants and contracts to other organizations to put emerging technologies to use in modern libraries and information systems.

Association of American Publishers
71 Fifth Avenue
New York, NY 10003

The Association of American Publishers (AAP), with more than 200 members located in every region of the United States, is the principal trade association of the book publishing industry. The Association's highest priorities are: Expanding domestic and foreign markets for American books, journals, and electronic publishing products; Promoting the status of Publishing in the United States and abroad; Defending intellectual freedom at home and the freedom of written expression worldwide; Keeping AAP member publishers informed on legislative, regulatory, and policy issues that affect our industry, and serving as the industry's voice on these issues; Protecting the rights of creators through ongoing efforts in defense of copyright; and Offering practical educational programs to assist members in the management of their companies.

This document was printed on DocuTech by Integrated Book Technology, Inc. The DocuTech Publishing System uses digital technology and prints documents at the rate of 135 pages a minute with a resolution of 600 dots per inch to provide high quality printed output.

The paper used in this publication meets the minimum requirements of the American National Standard for Information Sciences - Permanence of Paper for Printed Publications and Documents in Libraries and Archives, ANSI Z39.48-1992.

Library of Congress Cataloging-In-Publication Data

Librarians and publishers in the scholarly information process :
    transition in the electronic age : a report from the Joint Working
    Group on Professional and Scholarly Information in the Electronic
    Age / under the sponsorship of the Council on Library Resources and
    the Professional/Scholarly Publishing Division, Association of
    American Publishers, Inc.; report prepared by Linda Scovill.
        p. cm.
    Includes bibliographical references.
    ISBN 0-933636-30-X
    1. Libraries and publishing--United States. 2. Scholarly
publishing--United States. 3. Electronic publishing--United States.
I. Scovill, Linda. II. Joint Working Group on Professional and
Scholarly Information in the Electronic Age. III. Council on
Library Resources. IV. Association of American Publishers.
Professional/Scholarly Publishing Division.
Z716.6.L48 1994
070.5'94--dc20   94-48709
                                                           CIP

LIBRARIANS AND PUBLISHERS IN THE SCHOLARLY INFORMATION PROCESS:
Transition in the Electronic Age

Report prepared by:

Linda Scovill
Scovill, Paterson Inc.

Editor: Charles J. Lowry
Associate Editor: Lorna Petersen
Editorial Directors:
Barbara J. Meredith, AAP
W. David Penniman, CLR

Based on the work of members of the Joint Working Group on Professional and Scholarly Information in the Electronic Age under the sponsorship of the Council on Library Resources and the Professional/Scholarly Publishing Division, Association of American Publishers, Inc.

Janet D. Bailey	*Elsevier Science Inc.*
Betty Bengtson	*University of Washington, Seattle*
Harold Billings	*The University of Texas at Austin*
Robert D. Bovenschulte	*New England Journal of Medicine*
Robert T. Grant	*CRC Press, Inc.*
Margaret M. Irwin	*John Wiley and Sons*
Barbara J. Meredith	*Association of American Publishers*
Carol Hansen Montgomery	*Hahnemann University*
W. David Penniman	*Council on Library Resources, Inc.*
Sarah M. Pritchard	*Smith College*
John M. Saylor	*Engineering Library, Cornell University*
Linda Scovill	*Scovill, Paterson Inc.*
Robert Shirrell	*University of Chicago Press*
Elaine Sloan	*University Library, Columbia*
Facilitator Christine Harris	*Consultant*

We also acknowledge, with gratitude, contributions from:
Julia Blixrud   *Council on Library Resources*

CONTENTS

SITUATION ANALYSIS

Both academic librarians and professional/scholarly publishers exist within a scholarly community that values professional and scholarly information and has high expectations for its role in solving the human, social, scientific and cultural issues of our day. Yet, problems and controversies have led to tensions between librarians and publishers in recent years. Librarians, both generalists and specialists, are confronted with rising journal prices, especially in the sciences, an unremitting proliferation in the number and specialization of such journals, and the necessity of making large capital investments in both hardware and software, sometimes in the face of inadequate or even diminished support from public or university budgets. These burdens come on top of a general requirement of the library to maintain and expand traditional print collections, and of the librarian to keep abreast of developments in specific academic fields and of developments in new information technologies, as well as to keep the library open longer hours, offer an expanded array of services and retool staff members for a changing information environment.

At the same time, publishers have faced major investments in infrastructure and new technology to deliver information electronically to a small but increasing user base. At a time when the subscriber base for print journals is generally diminishing and has not yet been replaced by demand for electronic works, and while the library market for scholarly monographs is severely depressed, publishers seek to preserve operating income — sometimes by raising prices — to finance new works; to pay authors, editors and support staff; to pay for setting type, buying paper, printing, binding (or their electronic equivalents), marketing, fulfillment and distribution; to buy postage and word processors; to pay rent and subsidize new works. The publisher must also put into place and pay for its in-house editorial and production team, which ensures that published material meets appropriate standards of freshness, originality and importance in a well-designed and long-lasting physical format. All these factors are considered in making decisions about whether to publish a book or monograph, to launch a new journal or expand an existing one, or to raise or lower prices.

It is therefore not surprising that members of the scholarly community have different and often conflicting expectations about the intellectual property rights of information providers versus their own desire for immediate, high quality, low cost information that is quickly and easily accessed. Authors — both researchers and academics — understand the value of publication to professional advancement. They seek compensation through a mix of research grants, teaching or research salaries, and royalties or other forms of financial support by publishing. Publishers receive compensation primarily through subscriptions to journals from libraries and individuals, or from the sale of books or other (including electronic) publications and services to libraries, bookstores, wholesalers and individual users or from license fees for photocopying and other uses. They expect a positive return on their investment. Libraries are funded through the budgets of their parent institutions, and through grants and gifts; some are looking at providing some services for their clients for a fee, and at obtaining external funding for the start-up costs of new electronic services.

Classic market forces are coming into play: libraries are canceling subscriptions (not, however, without some counter pressure from their scholarly patrons) and looking to data bases and "on-demand" document delivery to supply access to particular information needed by their communities. Publishers are starting fewer new journals: from 3,200 new journals launched in 1980 to fewer than 1,000 by 1990.[1] Libraries have decreased purchases of scholarly monographs[2] in order to maintain subscription budgets. This force, coupled with a general trend favoring journal publication as the preferred medium for scholarly communication, has caused the monograph, a format traditionally used by scholars in the humanities and social sciences, nearly to disappear. One publisher noted that his company, which published four hundred monographs in 1989, would publish only forty in 1995. While some university press directors argue that the monograph is not dead and still has a prominent

---

[1] *Ulrich's International Periodicals Directory 1992-93,* 33rd Edition. New Providence, NJ: R. R. Bowker (1992), Preface.

[2] "Monograph" is variously defined by publishers and customers. While officially a learned treatise or book on a single or narrow topic, it is sometimes used to mean any book for practicing scholars or professionals (e.g. cardiologists, environmental planners) as opposed to a textbook for students. Sometimes it seems that if a book sells, it is called a "book" or "serious non-fiction." If it does not sell, it is called a "monograph."

role in some important publishing operations, others take the opposite view. Kenneth Arnold, formerly of Rutgers University Press, has announced that "the monograph as a viable economic base for university presses is now dead."[3] All agree that the average unit sales of monographs have declined dramatically. It is no surprise that the opposing dynamics of these forces have led to conflict marked by hard rhetoric.

Members of the Joint Working Group embarked on a study of the functions publishers and librarians perform, how each adds value to the information it handles, how key economic issues challenge both old and new ways of doing business, and how electronic delivery of information may change traditional roles and economics. Both publishers and librarians explored how each performs parallel but separate functions. For example, both carry out acquisitions, information management, marketing and distribution/dissemination functions. Most important, each group acknowledged that it knew less about the other's roles than previously thought. And, if publishers and librarians do not fully understand the others' work, then authors, scholars, researchers and university administrators are even less likely to realize the many steps in the publishing, distribution and storage of scholarly communication. We hope that one of the outcomes of this Joint Working Group will be a wider and fuller understanding by all segments of the academic community of the roles and tasks undertaken by publishers and librarians.

The Joint Working Group concluded that although the electronic age may change the *methods* by which these functions are performed, and in some cases who performs them, the scholarly community's need for these functions will remain. Indeed, in some cases the need may increase. Nonetheless, difficult economic issues and other challenges could limit publishers' and librarians' ability to realize the benefits of the new technologies.

The questions before the Joint Working Group then became how changes made possible by electronic publishing could be implemented in economically beneficial ways, either by changing the mix of functions, or by changing the information products, or by creating new working relationships

[3]Kenneth Arnold, "The Scholarly Monograph Is Dead, Long Live the Scholarly Monograph," *Scholarly Publishing on the Electronic Networks...Proceedings of the Second Symposium.* Washington, D.C.: Association of Research Libraries (1993), p. 75.

and alliances. The final question was deemed important as well: how to inform the other participants in the information cycle about what librarians and publishers contribute to the value of professional and scholarly information, both in traditional print and in electronic publications.

MISSION

In October, 1993 two organizations — the Council on Library Resources (Washington, DC) and the Professional/Scholarly Publishing Division of the Association of American Publishers (New York and Washington, DC) — agreed to co-sponsor a Joint Working Group on Professional and Scholarly Information in the Electronic Age. Appendix A on page 54 describes the project approved by the two organizations.

The Joint Working Group, consisting of equal numbers of professional and scholarly publishers and academic librarians, was asked to address common issues of value-added contributions in the emerging electronic environment, to identify the issues that need to be addressed for successful collaboration and to create and distribute a report summarizing its findings. Although this effort has concentrated on primary publishers and academic librarians, the Group has considered the entire chain, from researcher to end user, with all intermediate links including subscription agents, secondary publishers and on-line vendors and list servers. The focus of the group was on scholarly journals. Much of the deliberation, however, could be extended beyond, to monographs and even other forms of communication, including conferences and meetings.

The Joint Working Group first identified the value publishers and librarians add to scholarly and professional information. As the contributions of each are not widely understood within academic communities, the Group aimed to articulate the ways in which these contributions affect the process of distributing scholarly materials, what each entity adds, what special services each performs, and whether new models of scholarly communication will shift or eliminate some current services.

The second step was to identify issues that may help or hinder alliances with other segments of the scholarly communications process. New technologies may help redefine and remold traditional roles, but collaboration among different constituencies of the professional and scholarly communities rather than confrontation will likely prove the best path toward realizing electronic opportunities and benefits.

THE INFORMATION CYCLE AND ITS PARTICIPANTS

As Gordon Graham, editor of *Logos,* recently noted, "The Gutenbergian knowledge chain is roughly hexagonal: from author to publisher to printer to vendor to librarian to the reader, the ultimate consumer, who closes the loop with feedback to the author."[4]

Richard E. Lucier, University Librarian and Assistant Vice Chancellor for Academic Information Management at the University of California San Francisco, has presented a schematic of today's information cycle and suggested that the electronic age in some cases and in some disciplines could cause the cycle to be shortened and focused. The mechanism for this process would involve a collaborative group of information scientists, librarians, publishers, software engineers and others.[5]

Figure 1.

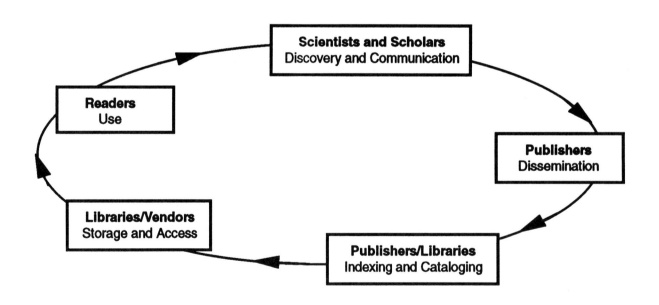

[4]Gordon Graham, *As I Was Saying,* London: Hans Zell, Publishers (1994), p. 145.

[5]These figures originally appeared in *Educom Review,* Volume 27, Number 6, p. 26 (November/December 1992). Mr. Lucier's article, from which these copyrighted slides have been excerpted with his kind permission, is entitled, "Towards a Knowledge Management Environment: A Strategic Framework."

Figure 2.

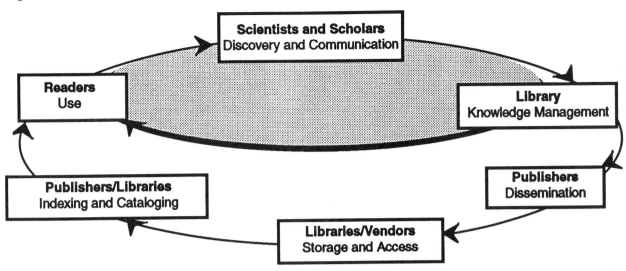

Those who seek economic relief from high costs (publishers) or high prices (libraries) have asked whether eliminating points of the information cycle could achieve their goals. We cannot begin to move toward these goals until we understand the functions each present participant performs.

As a scholarly work makes its way from researcher to end user, both librarians and publishers add value by increasing the breadth or depth of the work's utility, by altering raw material, by adding important information, by communicating its availability, by adding access points (e.g., indexing or abstracting), and by creating benefits for the customer. Quality, cost and availability combine to provide a measure of value,[6] which is recognized and validated by the customer's purchase or use of the information. Both libraries and publishers are struggling to understand how electronic publishing alternatives will raise, lower or simply transfer the costs of these additions to the value of the work to other participants.

[6]Paul Saffo, "Quality in an Age of Electronic Incunabula," *Liberal Education* Volume 79, Number 1 (Winter 1993), p. 22.

PUBLISHING

Information Functions

The Joint Working Group looked at the current publishing process and its functions and tasks as a first step in evaluating how this process may change in the electronic environment. The process includes development, authoring, formal and informal peer communication, editing and validation, assuming financial risk, design and production, communicating persuasively with the market, negotiating and ensuring the functions of ownership/privacy/security, and distribution. This sequence of steps is described below and also presented in a chart in Appendix C (page 63).

At a typical publishing house these functions may be shared among several areas, such as editorial/production, legal/financial/operations and marketing.[7]

The Value Publishers Add to Professional and Scholarly Information

The value added by the publishers lies in quality control through selection committees and peer review, quality control through editorial assistance and format standardization and quality control through high production standards. To this publishers add efficient and varied distribution channels and services, including sales and marketing, copyright protection and royalty payments.

---

[7]For example, "develop content" is listed on the chart in Appendix C as an editorial/production function. If, however, a professional publisher wanted to develop content for a new electronic database to be ordered and delivered online, marketing personnel might conduct research on content, packaging, pricing and acceptance; editorial/production personnel would add the results of their efforts to author, editor and reviewer input to make decisions about what information should be included, how it should be presented, and how it should be organized and indexed. Finally, the operations or MIS department might advise on how to help the content flow smoothly through electronic fulfillment and distribution systems.

The Joint Working Group identified specific publishers' added value as it relates to their information functions:

Editorial/Production:

> Selection and review (external peer review and internal contents review) of manuscripts provide quality control of the contents of publication and provide filters to help scholars winnow information.

> Editors' constant scanning and selection help identify and respond to emerging fields.

> Selection for publication also plays a major role in academic promotion and tenure systems and grant procurement, as an indicator of intellectual value or research quality.

> Content development organizes and enhances meaning, and may stimulate thought or provide an encyclopedic range and completeness of information by grouping different types of materials into one package.

> Editing of content, language/style and format ensures quality control in communicating ideas and data and supports and advances the creative process.

> Applying standards and style guides to material, including citations and presentation format, results in an orderly structure for the communication of scholarship.

> A combination of good peer and internal reviewing, editing, proofreading and making author corrections and revisions promotes accuracy of information.

> Effective visual design enhances readability and promotes facility in using publications.

> Effective management of typesetting, printing and binding processes provides quality control of the product.

> Publication can create an archive or authoritative article of record frozen in time, allowing researchers to test hypotheses and replicate and confirm results.

Indexing, soliciting and providing author-generated abstracts, and cataloguing at the time of publication all help readers, researchers and on-line vendors chart a path through large quantities of new material.

Legal/Financial/Operations:

Managing the financial risk of scholarly communication provides the investment necessary to complete the work. Economies of scale and efficient financial management help to reduce the cost of information.

Administration of author and other contracts creates a structure which is able to preserve the interests of the parties to the contract. The assignment of rights and licenses facilitates the spread of learning.

Royalties or grants to authors, institutions and learned societies support the creative, research and education processes.

Copyright administration and enforcement protect the creative process, preserve the integrity of the work and the rights of authors and publishers to receive compensation for their work, and provide a flexible legal framework for the wide dissemination of the work.

Centralized clearinghouses that negotiate permissions to copy or to use the work contain the cost of copyright administration and facilitate use by those seeking rights to use or distribute material.

Marketing:

The "Seal of Approval" or imprint based on the publisher's reputation and specialization helps customers select information.

Exclusive groupings of information — for example, producing catalogues by subject — help customers learn what is available in their fields.

Marketing and selling activities provide wide distribution of information, reaching a broader audience than is possible to those who self-publish.

The sale of rights or granting of licenses to publish in other languages or formats encourages the spread of learning worldwide.

Broad distribution of published works supports the democratic access to information.

Increased volume of sales may reduce the cost of each unit, whether book or journal, whether print or electronic.[8]

Economic Issues

The Joint Working Group looked at four basic economic questions for both publishers and librarians:

1.   Sources of revenues/funding and how costs are incurred/allocated;
2.   Accountability — to whom and for what;
3.   Other stakeholders and their needs and expectations;
4.   What is needed to succeed and thrive.

Financial terms vary between the two groups. Publishers speak of "revenue streams" or "sales"; librarians speak of "funding" or "allocations." Each means the money coming in. Similarly, publishers speak of how they "incur costs" or "expenses"; librarians speak of "expenditures." Each means the money going out. Finally, publishers may speak of "bottom line" or "profit (or loss) before tax" or "operating income" or "reinvestment" (non-profit publishers). Librarians may or may not have "unexpended funds." Each means what is left of revenues/funding after costs/expenditures are deducted.

Sources of revenues

Publishers' revenues come from sales of products to, or the right to use the product by, customers. Products may include books, journals and other serials, audiovisual materials, and

---

[8]Interestingly, a preliminary review of this list by a small panel consisting of scholars, publishers, librarians and academic administrators outside the Joint Working Group suggested that they do not perceive the legal/financial/operations functions as adding value for the user. This includes paying royalties and other grants to authors, institutions and learned socities. Enforcing, administering and containing the cost of copyright administration through a centralized clearinghouse may be more valued by authors whose works may otherwise be pirated, plagarized, copied or changed than by those who use the works. Managing financial risk and investment, i.e. underwriting the costs associated with the selection, production and distribution of scholarly work, was not perceived by the panel as an activity that added value for the user, although without it, many publications would not exist. Nor, in spite of the axiom to "publish or perish," did the panel see or value the publisher's role in supporting scholars' promotion and tenure system or grant procurement as a benefit to the user of the information.

electronic publications. Journal revenues may be based primarily on subscriptions, with or without advertising, or journals may be distributed to readers at no cost but be fully subsidized by the advertisers ("controlled circulation journals"). Most scholarly journals are subscription based, and that is the model considered here. On average, subscription-based journals derive about 75% of their revenues from subscriptions, with 15% coming from advertising, 3% from the page and submissions fees charged by some journals, and the balance of 7% from miscellaneous other revenues, including author reprints, copyright fees and individual copy sales.[9]

Copyright administration and rights sales may include user fees, on-line fees or copying fees for journals, as well as subsidiary, translation, paperback and broadcast/film or magazine serialization rights for books. The revenues resulting from these sales are used to pay authors, to pay publication costs, to invest in new products and to provide a return on the publisher's investment ("ROI"). Some university presses and scholarly societies also receive funds or subsidies from universities (either direct dollars or indirect support, such as office space), grants and foundations and/or membership dues.

Publishers lose sales revenues and licensing income when their publications are extensively photocopied without reimbursement, or when used books are resold (a phenomenon that has transformed the economics of textbook publishing), or when books are pirated abroad.

[9]Committee on Scholarly Journals, *1991 Survey of University Press Journals: A Survey of Journals Published by Member and Affiliate Presses of the Association of American University Presses*, New York: Association of American University Presses, p. 10 lists subscription revenues at 73.9%, advertising revenues at 3%, page charges at 7% and other revenues at 28.6%. *AAP Journal Publishers Survey:1984*, p. 1 lists subscription revenues for publisher-owned journals at 72%, advertising revenues at 17.7%, page charges and submission fees at 2.4%, and other revenues at 7.9%. The same *Survey* listed subscription revenues for journals controlled by scholarly associations or societies as 59%, reflecting the discounted subscription rates for members. Advertising revenues were 29.7%, page charges 1.8% and other revenues were 9.5%. An informal and unpublished updating of the AAP's 1984 *Survey*, conducted by members of the Joint Working Group, showed subscriptions to be 77.2% of revenues, advertising at 14.5%, page charges and fees at 2.8% and other revenues at 5.5%.

In the publishing industry, as in many industries, the "80:20 Rule" is commonly held to be true: for most publishers, twenty percent of their products produce eighty percent of their sales.[10] It does not, however, follow that a publishing program can encompass only that twenty percent. New publications may take time to get established. Sales of older, backlist publications — especially books — diminish over time. Indeed, the sales curve for virtually all publications begins to decline long before backlisting, which usually occurs a year after publication. Over all, more than half of all books published lose money. For journals, it is more common now than in the past that some journals publish at a loss, and even journals that are eventually profitable can take as long as five years to reach profitability. Predicting which ones will reach their sales and profit goals, and which will not, is very difficult, if not impossible. Books and journals that lose money are subsidized by other sources or products, and this has led some publishers to publish more books to spread the risk — a strategy that has not always paid off.

Publishers' expectations differ as to how soon a publication should pay for itself, break even and generate income in excess of costs. Scholarly and professional publishers commonly set their prices based on a mix of factors, such as the prices of competing products, the size of the potential market, the mix of distribution channels, their assumptions about how many copies or subscriptions they will sell, their projected costs and need for income to invest in new programs. Usually each new book is treated as a separate project, expected to pay for itself and then make a profit in its first and sometimes only printing over a relatively short time span (for commercial publishers, less than one year). The more "monographic" the book, the smaller the print run, the higher the price, and often, the longer the time it takes to break even and then sell out the first printing. Sixty to seventy percent of a monograph's sales occur in the first twelve months after publication. But the last thirty to forty percent may stretch over many years, reducing profitability. This makes a high initial sales curve, followed by an equally steep decline to flat and/or minimal sales over time. In contrast, high

---

[10]This is not the same thing, however, as eighty percent of their profits. While most publishers hope that their bestsellers are very profitable, especially in the book business, a bestseller may be sold at a small margin or have high on-going costs. While bestsellers are the "stars" of the famous Boston Study Group matrix, sometimes lesser sellers make up the "cash cows."

level textbooks for professionals or scholars in training, and reference works, tend to have a flatter, shorter curve in relation to anticipated new editions, which are more predictable over time.

As scholars and researchers have become increasingly specialized over the last three decades, dividing into smaller and smaller "niche" groups, the number of potential readers for any given treatise has declined. At the same time a growing population of researchers and scholars of all types who seek to publish their research has increased the number of monographs submitted to publishers. When accepted for publication, these new monographs have had higher prices as publishers seek to recover costs from a smaller number of units sold. Libraries — the traditional "first customer" of monographs — have not had the budgets to keep up. Further, "timeliness" is the watchword of science. Darwin today would not be able to spend thirty years refining *Origin of Species* before launching his theory of evolution. In today's world he would have staked out his claims in a series of short journal articles, because the journal is the vehicle for communicating new information. In Darwinian terms, then, the traditional scholarly monograph or learned treatise on a single subject has not proved sufficiently adaptable to avoid the threat of extinction.

How costs are incurred or allocated

Not-for-profit monograph publishers generally allocate their sales revenues along the following lines:[11]

Authors	15%
Editorial expense	15%
Production cost	30%
Marketing and advertising	10%
Distribution	10%
Administrative, rent	10%
	90%

This accounts for 90% of revenues, leaving 10% for "reinvestment." Commercial publishers, of course, need to do better in order to pay taxes, reinvest and receive a possible return on their investment.

[11]From the President, "Where Does the Money Go (and Where Does It Come From)?" *CLR Reports,* New Series, Number 3 (January 1994), p. 1.

New journals and large reference book projects usually take some years to reach profitable sales levels. Continuing projects such as these tend to develop a consistent sales history over time that makes it somewhat easier to estimate the number of subscribers and the resulting revenue stream. Publishers and professional associations frequently use profits from other projects to underwrite the costs of a new journal for a period of as long as five years, until the break-even point is reached. In the best scenario, that new journal will reach profitability and then begin to subsidize other new efforts. In the worst case, it is a loss, draining funds from other projects, although for-profit publishers may be able to deduct some parts of the loss before taxes.

Journal costs are incurred or allocated along lines similar to the previous example.

Editorial expense[12]	22%
Production costs	24%
Marketing	12%
Fulfillment and distribution	10%
Administrative, rent	18%

This accounts for 86% of revenues, leaving 14% before taxes for reinvestment, both for new product development and to undertake the research, development and equipment costs associated with entering an electronic publishing milieu. This does not take into account any return on the shareholders' investment.

The "immovable object" of publishing costs is subsidizing the "first copy" of a book or journal — all the costs before the printing press begins to run. These development costs often clash with the irresistible market forces of price sensitivity. They include all editing, manuscript development, design, keyboarding, and art (photographs, illustrations, charts and tables, drawings) costs, including advance payments to book authors who are still writing their manuscripts. In the final accounting, if a publisher spends $50,000.00 (of course, multimedia and/or CD-ROM publication "first copy" costs can be much higher) for these pre-printing costs, and plans to sell 500 units, each unit will include $100.00 in its price to cover just these costs (and more for the printing, marketing

[12]Includes royalties and other grants and editorial fees to university-based editors or to learned socities, plus publisher's editorial labor and copy editing.

and distribution of the product). At 5,000 units planned to be sold, the price will include $10.00 for pre-printing costs. And for a very few consumer products (the *New York Times* hard cover bestseller lists, for example), where 50,000 units may be sold, the price will include $1.00 to cover pre-printing costs.

This is the hard rock that will not be crushed by distributing information electronically. Although there may be some savings in individual steps of the pre-printing process (by editing and preparing copy from author disks, for example), and in distribution, the effect on the overall "first copy" cost will not be large because the process will require many of the same steps and highly trained professional personnel to create the product as traditional methods required. Some new methods of manuscript preparation and production may even require *more* steps and/or personnel. To impose a statistical perspective, if a monograph publisher saved 10% on production costs by automating pre-print activities, and production costs accounted for 30% of the total costs of publishing the monograph, then the overall savings for that monograph would be 3% (10% of 30%) — not a material cost savings.

If publishers produce books and journals on line (or as a "stream" of material or chapters rather than a "package" of a finite number of chapters, articles or pages), once again the cost will decrease only slightly because most of the cost is incurred "up front." Similarly, if librarians and end users "purchase" on-line books only when they print out pages at their local PC, those few pages printed out (based on the 80:20 rule to the *nth* power) will have to carry the full burden of the costs of getting all the material on line at the pre-printing stage. It would seem to follow that the price per page in this scenario would grow exponentially, and probably extend well beyond the financial resources of individual purchasers. What is so far unknown is whether usage over time would increase sufficiently to spread the costs over a larger number of PC-printed "units." Thus, it is interesting that an internal study conducted at AT&T showed that demand for internally generated technical documents ebbed within a year after publication, until information about them was provided at the researchers' desktop computers. Then demand extended to material five years old and beyond. This could have interesting implications for publishers' markets and pricing structures.

Accountability — to whom and for what

A commercial press is accountable to the owner of the business, whether that is an individual, association, institution or group of shareholders. Its officers are accountable for a fair rate of return on investment, which is defined in various ways, but at the minimum should be greater than investors would get if they put their money into a bank (investor risk is a part of the equation here). In today's business climate, many shareholders of large publishing corporations look for a return of 10% - 14% on their stock investment, consisting of a combination of the appreciation of the price of the stock and its paid dividends. Like other large corporate entities, publicly held publishers are also under pressure to deliver favorable returns on a quarterly basis.

University presses are accountable to their universities and boards of trustees. It is often assumed that university presses are accountable to their faculties to publish their works, but few university presses have more than a third of their authors from their own institutions, and the largest ones have even fewer. While university presses are "not-for-profit" for tax purposes, this does not mean that they manage their business to "break even." The larger university presses are asked to provide income or "contributions" to their sponsoring institutions, and that trend is growing among medium sized university presses as well. University presses usually must find their own funding to invest in new products. More and more universities are unwilling to subsidize the presses that lose money, although many indirect subsidies can occur in a campus setting.

Scholarly societies are accountable to their members, and along lines similar to the university presses. They are more likely than for-profit publishers to charge authors a per page fee to publish, a part of the revenue "mix" that allows societies to offer their members special, lower subscription prices. Publications of the learned societies may account for up to seventy percent of the societies' revenues,[13] with meetings and conferences (including seminars and continuing education) the second large piece and membership dues a small percentage of the total income. Society publishers are especially accountable to providing their members with a price benefit for their publications. This is

[13]"Publishing and Society Goals," Concurrent Session I, 14th Annual Meeting, Society for Scholarly Publishing, Chicago (June 18, 1992).

one of the factors that has led to multi-tiered pricing for individual (member or non-member) and institutional subscribers.

Other stakeholders, their needs and expectations

All publishers are accountable to their authors and their customers and, in a different way, to their employees and suppliers.

Publishers need to do a good job for their authors, to present their information fairly, accurately, effectively and attractively, and to market their work well. Failure to do so results in disgruntled authors, who can ruin a publisher's reputation in the marketplace. Thus there is a parallel between the need for publishers to satisfy their authors and the need for librarians to satisfy their faculties, just as there is a parallel between the need for publishers to satisfy their customers and librarians to satisfy their readers. The publisher's perceived visibility and status in the marketplace influences the scholar's or researcher's perceived status. Effective marketing leads to high visibility and happy authors.

Publishers are accountable to customers for the quality of their products, for informing customers, including secondary publishers, about product content, price and availability, and for timely and cost effective delivery in good condition. When the customers are bookstores, wholesalers or subscription agents, the publisher develops a marketing partnership with the bookseller to reach the end-user.

Finally the publisher is accountable to its employees for compensation, job satisfaction and career development, and to its suppliers for business with timely payment.

What is needed to succeed or survive

Growth is the key to success. Growth in overall revenues at a greater rate than expenses is essential for the success of any publisher.

A happy match between product and market — the outcome of good editorial and marketing judgment — and good customer service leads to success. A growing market is a big help, as is an understanding of what influences users' interest in information. Timing is often an important variable, as is presentation and access to distribution channels (an issue, for example, in selling CD-ROM disks, which are only just beginning to be distributed through some bookstores). When markets are declining, prices may initially increase, because costs are spread over fewer units. Survival then becomes an issue. The number of publications in a field may decrease, while those that remain are offered at higher prices.

Long-term success depends on profitable growth (or a positive "contribution" or "reinvestment" fund in not-for-profit terms). This means selling more units of each book or journal title, constantly improving the sales of the top titles while publishing fewer that drain the fiscal resources of the company. A good balance of providing customers with the information they need and providing investors with a fair return on investment is the key to success. Sound financial management that improves profitability through a positive price:cost ratio also helps publishers continue to produce the return expected by their owners. Timing, adaptability and sufficient capital are key risk/survival/success issues in the rapidly changing environment. These realities pertain both to commercial publishers and to the not-for-profits. Although they may measure financial results differently, they face the same constraints, restrictions and expectations. This point needs to be emphasized and repeated.

LIBRARIES

Information Functions

Just as in the case of publishers, the Joint Working Group also looked at current information processes in libraries and how they function. The process includes identification and selection of information; information organization and management; interpretation and dissemination of information to users; and collection management, archiving and preservation (see Appendix D, page 64). In a typical academic library, these functions would be performed by a variety of departments.

The Value Librarians Add to Professional and Scholarly Information

The value added by libraries is in selection and acquisition, organization, access and reference services, preservation of scholarly materials and promotional and training activities. Without the subscription fees, book purchases, and licensing income from libraries, publishers would not be able to produce new works.

The Joint Working Group identified libraries' added value as it relates to the information functions they perform:

**Identification of
Users' Needs:**

Screening of many publications results in collections that best fit users' needs.

Specialization/reputation of the library may help scholars select information.

Creation of intellectually coherent collections assists scholars in their research and in understanding the growth of a field.

Book or other publication reviews written by librarians for the reviewing media provide professional critical analysis and aid scholars and peers in the selection of published works.

Ongoing direct communication with users informs librarians as they select materials and as they communicate further with publishers about gaps which new publishing products might fill.

Information Organization:

Library purchase of publications reduces the cost of information for students and scholars.

Selection of titles and creation of search mechanisms provide filters to help scholars winnow information.

Library information services, cataloging and various searching systems enable access to information by various avenues, e.g., author, subject.

Groupings of information by content and format organize knowledge and provide a structured information system and guides to collection management and development.

Public Services:

Scholars' free use of libraries supports democratic access to information.

Broad network of academic libraries provides wide distribution of information to both experts and non-experts, and to a larger audience than is available through other distribution channels.

Professional assistance and searching systems direct people to appropriate sources. Librarians' active consultation and guidance assist information searches, analyze and critique information sources and expose or convert people to new information.

Professional librarians may also find and synthesize information for people, and develop new secondary and tertiary information tools.

Librarians teach and train users to find and organize their own information, to understand the communication and publication patterns of disciplines and to develop strategies for information analyses. Librarians have primary responsibility for the information literacy of their users. They develop multiple strategies for accomplishing this, including actively integrating this teaching within the university's curricula.

Both physical and virtual libraries provide a single point of access for information.

Collection Management:

Archiving of information preserves the records of culture and scholarship, as well as the preservation and/or conservation of artifact, providing housing for collections; shelving and organizing improve access for scholars; making decisions about what to preserve for future generations of scholars helps to shape our cultural heritage.

Economic Issues

University librarians have noted that both they and end users may well have only very partial ideas of publishers' cost factors in scholarly publication.[14] Professional and scholarly publishers, who have long been aware of budget constraints in library purchases of print materials, want to know more about the trends of economic measures relating to libraries generally, and in relation to their scientific, technical and medical collections and services.

Sources and allocation of funding

A recent study[15] has shown a general deterioration in the financial support provided to university library budgets. Still, as the Working Group discussed, eighty percent or more of a university library's funds comes from the institution's budget. Of that, up to about ten percent may come from endowments specific to the library. Grants, foundations, contracts and gifts may contribute up to twenty percent, but competition for such funds is growing. When grants and gifts are received, they tend to be used for special purchases, and not for core functions. Some library services — such as photocopying, fees for service, and fines on overdue circulated materials — may generate revenues. In a tight budget, these activities, which generate less than ten percent of the library's total funding, receive a lot of attention as areas of potential development.

Faced with a limited pie, librarians have turned to productivity gains by employing fewer people or by making programmatic cuts in an effort to release money for other purposes. Figure 3

[14]Robert Wedgeworth, "Remaking Scholarly Publishing," *The Chronicle of Higher Education,* Volume 40, Number 17 (December 15, 1993), p. 15.

[15]Kendon Stubbs, "Trends in Unversity Funding for Research Libraries," *ARL* (January 1994), pp. 1-3.

illustrates the allocation of the "pie" across general categories of expenditures for libraries in higher education.[16] According to the recently released study of university libraries by the Andrew W. Mellon Foundation, "Salaries have fallen steadily, from an average of 62 percent of total expenditures in 1963 to 52% in 1991."[17] Allocations for library mat... ... ... around thirty percent, and general and administrative costs, equipment, communications services (cicip... online charges, postage) and preservation take more of the library's budget. Often, interlibrary loan, computer search charges, etc., formerly budgeted under operations or supplies or "other" now have increasing and flexible budget lines of their own; contract services account for the balance.

Figure 3

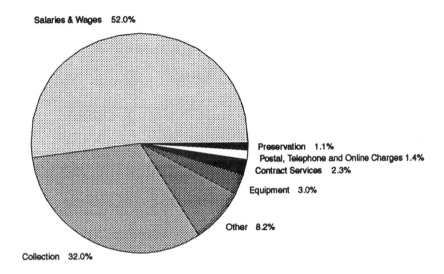

It would be good for the library community to develop a formal study of how libraries allocate funds by function. On an informal basis, the library members of the Joint Working Group suggested that the costs of providing public services (reference, access, interlibrary loan and collection development) and technical services (ordering and processing materials, cataloguing, preservation) are roughly equal and together account for up to eighty percent of the total budget.

[16]Jeffrey Williams, "Academic Libraries: 1990," E.D. TABS, National Center for Education Statistics, U.S. Department of Education, Office of Educational Research and Improvement. December 1992 (NCES 93-044).

[17]Anthony M. Cummings, Marcia L. Little, William G. Bowen, Laura O. Lazarus, and Richard H. Ekman, "University Libraries and Scholarly Communication." A Study Prepared for the Andrew W. Mellon Foundation and published by the Association of Research Libraries (1992).

The cost of materials (publications) is part of the cost of providing public services. As W. David Penniman has noted,[18]

> The cost of materials, though only one portion of a library's overall budget, has attracted much attention. With high fixed costs for other budgetary items, the variable cost of material expenditures takes on even more attention. With spiraling costs for some journals and tense relations between publishers and librarians, the search for alternatives is intense, and current journal pricing is perceived as a bottleneck — this bottleneck must also include the price placed on intellectual property and its protection....

> Elimination of local holdings for economic or other reasons creates a bottleneck of accessibility by traditional methods. Will the journal or monograph be available, if sought by other means at other locations? This, of course, assumes that the user will turn to the library for access, not necessarily a good assumption based on past user studies. Therefore, accessibility is a bottleneck with many dimensions....

When materials *prices* go up faster than materials *budget allocations*, librarians seek options to resolve the difference. These have included:

1. Eliminating or postponing the purchase of scholarly monographs in order to maintain journals collections.

   This option has been so widely exercised over the last two decades that the market for and publication of scholarly monographs has dramatically declined (see pages 2-3).

2. Canceling subscriptions, based on
   a. Eliminating collections of journals not frequently used;
   b. Providing access to the information through increased interlibrary loans and/ or the use of commercial document delivery services, through resource sharing among a group of collaborative libraries, or through licensing of electronic access and transmission of information on local or wide area networks.

   A 1993 study published by the Association of Research Libraries[19] documented the full — and high — costs of interlibrary loans to users and lenders. The study could lead librarians to reevaluate usage levels in relation to subscription price, to increased use of document delivery services as a cost effective alternative to traditional interlibrary loan, and to greater demand for electronic information products and services.

3. Preferring and promoting new pricing models, such as transaction-based pricing or site licensing, for electronically delivered information.

---

[18]W. David Penniman, "Visions of the Future: Libraries and Librarianship for the Next Century," The Fifth Nasser Sharif Lecture, Pratt Graduate School of Information and Library Science, New York (April 8, 1994), pp. 5-6.

[19]Marilyn M. Roche, *ARL/RLG Interlibrary Loan Cost Study--A Joint Effort by the Association of Research Libraries and the Research Libraries Group,* Washington, D.C.: Association of Research Libraries (1993).

This is not an immediate solution, but a long-range possibility. Systems and policies are still in their infancy, as both librarians and publishers hope that collaborative studies of technology and usage, some of them already in progress, will answer the many technical and economic questions surrounding setting up new ways to price information.

4. Seeking additional funding from government and private sector grants, from endowments and gift funds, and from revenue generating activities, such additional funds to be used for the purchase of materials.

Libraries have not to date preferred this option because increasing competition among higher education institutions for such funds means that libraries cannot count on higher levels of income from such sources.

An interesting productivity and personnel trend is that public service functions are requiring more skilled, professional staff as technical services functions shift more to support staff or are even outsourced. As librarians have asked themselves, "Why do we do this particular activity?" they have targeted technical services as the source of headcount cuts and increased productivity, eliminating some traditional functions. There are some special challenges to doing so. While two-thirds of a university library's employees may have consisted of non-professional support staff, there has traditionally been little turnover in these positions and great resistance to change. In public universities support staff are likely to be civil service and/or unionized employees. Yet, as in most industries, the lower level and less skilled jobs have been eliminated more rapidly than high skilled or professional jobs. As technical services jobs and staff are eliminated, this value added may be "lost." But it is also possible that new kinds of technical service functions may develop and grow to serve the electronic environment.

Allocations for automation, including capital investment in computers and other equipment, are increasing more rapidly (albeit from a tiny base) than any other budget area. Automation costs today may represent up to twenty-five percent of the total library budget. This allocation includes services from groups such as OCLC or intra-institutional groups such as a university computer center. Finally, there is a steady five to ten percent of costs associated with administration, including staff training.

Accountability — to whom and for what

Accountability in library circles determines who in the academic community influences purchases. Librarians have many masters. They may be accountable to university administrators, faculty, boards (regents, trustees), donors and — in the case of public universities — legislators. Libraries' financial accountability to university administrators or their governing boards is to stay within budget and to manage their funds reasonably and effectively. The quality of a university library's collection and services is central to the faculty's teaching and research. The faculty are a powerful constituency and at some universities decide how the library's materials budget is spent. In other institutions, librarians make purchasing decisions, but usually with significant faculty input. Reporting may occur to various governing boards of the library and the university, and to the governing boards of regional and national accrediting and standards agencies. Regional and national accrediting agencies review university library systems, a key part of a school's overall accreditation. Federal and state legislatures mandate certain public university management auditing/accounting systems. University libraries may be accountable to legislatures and/or private donors to ensure that money has been well spent. Donors and foundations also often have interests and expectations concerning the excellence, reputation and quality of the institution, and may require acknowledgment in the form of the naming of buildings or collections or in other forms of public recognition.

Other stakeholders, their needs and expectations

Students are the largest group of other stakeholders, with marked influence on library hours, study space and service allocations. Many students, and generally the parents of students, may be more interested in the libraries' technological capabilities and collections. Alumni have expectations regarding the prestige of their university libraries and the maintenance of traditional collections, and they too look for access to library collections and new technology. Local community taxpayers also want access and expect "more for less" in relation to the taxes they are willing to pay. Consortial colleagues expect prompt response to interlibrary loan requests and, increasingly, collaborative involvement in networked information and shared resources agreements.

The professional community of librarians looks to university librarians to provide leadership in special projects, especially in preservation, new technology and cooperative resource development.

What is needed to succeed or survive

Success in today's university library environment lies in increased services that meet the needs and expectations of this broad range of stakeholders, the effective use of new technologies, and increased staff productivity. For example, in 1984, the Hahnemann University medical library conducted between 1,000 and 1,500 mediated searches a year. By 1994, on Medline alone there were between 1,000 and 1,500 mediated searches *a month*. Other libraries have installed CD-Rom databases and direct user access to networked databases to meet user needs; as a result, the number of *unmediated* searches has increased, while the number of mediated searches has plummeted.

Survival, in a time when universities' fiscal resources are strained,[20] demands that libraries maintain their traditional services and collections even as they use technology in new ways to deliver services and provide access to information on networks or through document delivery services (rather than developing additional physical collections). Managing budgets well and educating the stakeholders to perceive libraries and their services as essential to the institution are key survival skills for library executives. Effective public relations, communication and information on library services is part of this educational outreach. Libraries today also need to develop credibility in delivering services efficiently and to be proactive in providing new services that other institutions or departments cannot or do not provide. Librarians need to anticipate customer needs — for example, archiving of electronic materials. As one client noted, some day if the scientists don't use it, the historians will. And finally, library survival rests on the foundation of meeting accreditation standards.

---

[20]Although we do not, in this report, discuss facilities maintenance as a drain on library budgets, the library director still must compete for these funds against other institutional priorities. Although it is unclear how an electronic (or, more realistically, a combination paper/electronic) collection might alter traditional assumptions about facilities maintenance, librarian members of the joint working group pointed out that both traditional collections (with, usually, older facilities and greater space, shelving and storage requirements) and newer collections (with extensive rewiring and heavier electrical and/or communications infrastructure) require expensive physical arrangements.

HOW FUNCTIONS AND ADDED VALUE CHANGE IN THE ELECTRONIC ENVIRONMENT

The benefits of electronic publishing include increased speed of publication[21] and ease of soliciting user feedback, which can be incorporated into or tagged to appear next to the original work. Electronic publication provides the potential for reinventing traditional peer review by making it practical for subscribers to volunteer their services as reviewers.

Even when the final product is a print publication, electronic technology for editing and production functions, e.g. capturing authors' keystrokes, editing on line or on disk, typesetting, and producing / printing / duplicating / copying information, may ease production, require less labor and reduce costs in the production process. What it does *not* do is significantly reduce the "first copy" costs, the expense and labor required before the first article and/or journal issue is, in traditional terms, "released" to the production department for typesetting and printing. Similarly, electronic production requires personnel with a large amount of training in many technical fields, probably better trained and better paid than the personnel required for traditional print publishing. Twenty years ago copy editors may have known the *Chicago Manual of Style* from front to back. They edited and marked up manuscript in pencil or washable green ink. Today they still know the *Chicago Manual of Style*, equations and so forth, but the publisher must hire or train a "Tek" person to edit math articles written in Tek, and other people with special (and higher cost) computer skills for other subjects or applications.

Electronic information is potentially easy to change, use and publish in a wide variety of formats. It offers extraordinary opportunities for developing new kinds of searching engines, both within an original work and at the library level. Finally, it is cheaper to store information electronically, which reduces demands on libraries for additional "shelf" or storage space. Obsolescence and

---

[21]When, for example, *The On-Line Journal of Current Clinical Trials* was published by AAAS, it claimed to "publish" an article within forty-eight hours of acceptance.

technological advancement are, however, issues which must be considered in evaluating the economics of electronic storage. As an alternative to physical storage, electronic storage becomes one answer to the question of where the archiving and preservation of the scholarly tradition should occur. Another possibility is that libraries might develop collaborative contracts with publishers, by which the publishers maintain the archive of their own publications. This would require a change of function for the publishers, and possibly added expense.

Some characteristics of electronic publishing are more ambiguous. This ambiguity can stem from several factors: the number of potential "self-publishers" with access to networks, the interactive nature of certain electronic forms, the potentially public, i.e. networked, nature of many of the steps in the publishing process, e.g. peer review and commentary. In short, in an electronic environment, the authorship, identity and ownership of a work can become less clear because of the collaborative efforts to create it and the multiple inputs to construct it. The digital environment means that every copy is a technological equal of the original. Absent printed output, content may exist without form. Paper becomes an interface, a volatile, disposable medium for viewing information on demand, or a storage medium. It no longer serves a primary function as a communications medium. That attribute is performed by the computer's monitor screen.

The PC has made "desktop publishing" an option for any author, researcher, scientist, scholar, student or lay person (with or without true expertise in scholarly fields). This ease of entry to "publishing" or self-publishing, the existing lack of standards, and the variety of outputs of multiple databases may create information overload, thus increasing demands on librarians to filter and select from much more material.

Electronic publication sometimes replaces, sometimes supplements and sometimes parallels traditional print publication. It may shorten the distance, smooth the path or offer alternate routes between researcher and end user, but it will not eliminate the need for the functions now performed by publishers and librarians which add value to the scholarly communications process. Nonetheless, the electronic environment will change financial, technological and intellectual functions and value added activities.

Financial/legal changes

High on both librarians' and publishers' "wish lists" is that electronic publication will reduce their costs or transfer them elsewhere. Will the electronic revolution cut costs for both publishers and librarians? A newsletter issued by the Council on Library Resources[22] noted that

> Any new system must be compared to the baseline of our current system to see if the cost is really being reduced....For example, the cost of printing is being offset by the cost of each user having and using a display device (and often a printer, as well) to replace traditional "printing."

> Another interesting trade-off has to do with the cost of "fair use." Current product pricing takes into account *pro bono* or "fair use" costs. In other words, someone always pays for fair use. The same will have to be true in the future. Who will be asked to absorb the cost of fair use in the future? Why, those who foot the bill for the emerging process, of course.

> Sooner or later the cost of any service gets back to the customer (or someone footing the bill for the customer), and right now the customer is the library. Who will it be in the future? And who will foot the bill?

Changing markets and changes in technology require a much larger scale of capital investment in hardware and software and highly skilled staff than traditional print publication. Hybrid publication systems require costly parallel paths of paper and electronic publishing. The majority of costs for acquisition, peer review, editing and conversion of text and illustrations into a digitized format are still required for all of the equivalent electronic methods of dissemination, and will, in fact, require redesigning work flow. It will be interesting to see if public entities and universities, which now assume much of the costs of computer networks, will be willing or able to continue to assume the costs of modernization and operation.

Therefore the need for publishers (alone or together with others) to take and manage the financial risk of publishing, and its added value to everyone in the information cycle, could increase. We have seen that publishers add value to the process by managing financial transactions on behalf of the author. Will an author, given the choice of working with an established publisher and collecting royalties, prefer instead to self-publish on an electronic network and either forego financial compensation or attempt to enforce compensation from users? Will authors wish to handle complex

[22]From the President, "Where Does the Money Go (and Where Does It Come From)?" *CLR Reports,* New Series, Number 3 (January 1994), p. 2.

intellectual property rights negotiations themselves? Royalties and other payments to people for the fruits of their creative process are expected to remain valued, at least by their recipients; still, new mechanisms for payment may occur, such as transaction-based royalties, works for hire or one-time fees, or demands from self publishers for fees to be paid through new "shareware" mechanisms and credit cards.

This will lead to changes and additional complexity in administering and enforcing copyright, with new ways of compensating the creators of works and assigning ownership. Some participants in the information cycle ask whether copyright management could be used to reduce acquisition costs, for example by considering scholarly publications as "works for hire" from faculty members and research staff, with copyright belonging to and being administered and enforced by universities, which would expand "fair use" and "free" publication over the Internet or local networks. Others believe such a move would decrease the royalties and other payments to authors, while at the same time increasing the administrative costs and burdens placed on universities for rights and permissions. All of this would be unaccompanied by any increase in subscription or other income. Publishers would argue that voluntary action on the part of academic authors to retain their own copyrights and to grant publishers one-time rights to publishing their articles has the potential to destroy the scholarly communication process because of the increased complexity and costs for negotiation of rights,[23] and because limited licenses reduce publishers' opportunities to gain additional revenue from a particular work to help offset costs. Thus limited licenses would tend to drive up prices or eliminate some publications.

Licensing arrangements are likely to change and expand in any case. They are effective to the extent they define user communities for client services or marketing needs, or expand the applications and reach of scholarly works. But they can be misapplied to enhance dominant positions or restrict access to information. Some copyright clearance centers administer compulsory licenses, a controversial option in the U.S. It is generally agreed, however, that if any licensing process is overcomplicated, it will be costly and may not prevent abuses such as unauthorized use, redistribution, etc.

[23]Scott Bennett, "Copyright and Innovation in Electronic Publishing: A Commentary," *Journal of Academic Librarianship*, Volume 19, Number 2 (May 1993), p. 89.

We have seen that journals pricing remains a key issue for librarians. The electronic age may create new pricing models for information, such as those being tested by the TULIP Project (see Appendix E, p. 65). Prices could be based, as they now are, on a subscription model. Some "subscribers" want access to all that is available, while others want only one or two articles from a journal or pages from a book in a year.

That leads to document delivery and other transaction-based models (with or without free "browsing"), which meet the demand to pay for only what is used, but are costly to develop and administer by publishers and librarians. Although computer technology provides a practical means for auditing (and therefore charging) as well as tracking each discrete use of information and each information user, publishers do not yet have the sufficient experience to know how to price information "by the piece." It is unclear whether selling by the article is economically feasible. Transaction-based models may or may not allow free "browsing." Keeping the meter ticking may inhibit the time spent exploring information sources; the meter's not ticking may lead to a waste of resources. Any transaction-based model raises the question: if libraries and users buy one item at a time, will the volume of these transactions be sufficient to cover the cost of origination for a range of items (such as journal articles), including those not "bought" at all? Financial risk is currently spread across all items.

The question returns to one of who will fund research into alternative pricing structures (e.g., TULIP), electronic access, and the technological development of the infrastructure? All parties to the debate suggest "deep pocket organizations," which are any except their own.

Some librarians suggest eliminating bound, catalogued journals at the local level by offering information to end users on line from a central source. Others suggest — and are implementing — "deselection." They assert that scholars are fed up with the cost, inflexibility and inadequacy of print products. They want to distinguish "crucial" journals and decide which other sources need to be replaced, perhaps by identifying groups of scholars to create electronic alternatives to expensive journals (a competitive goal routinely assumed by publishers to be part of the editorial acquisition process).

Still others advocate an incremental pricing model, such as that used for mass paperbacks or microfilm, where the original print format is priced to carry pre-publication costs. Such a model would probably assume a time lag in electronic publication to allow publishers to recover first-copy costs. Among other forces is the increasing attention to the cost of sharing. As an example, a recent study by ARL/RLG[24] identified the cost of inter-library loan activity to both borrower and lender. As a result of this study, libraries are beginning to reevaluate their resource sharing policies and practices.

Technological changes

Those involved in the scholarly communication process need to find ways to decide what information to put on electronic networks, CD-ROMs or other systems, and how to manage, provide access to and license data use in a way that protects the producer. For example, some publishers are investigating what happens when a library licenses electronic tapes from individual publishers and makes them available through its own interfaces.[25]

Scholars will need electronic "super-catalogues" and multi-level catalogues that incorporate full-texts, standardized access points, and a bibliographic place holder. Almost every user of Internet complains about "junk overload," and as yet unmet needs to sort, organize and index new information sources. Much electronic information seeks users, instead of users seeking information. Therefore, how will the sorting of information be performed, and by whom? This is a role traditionally performed by librarians.

Computer-maintained individual profiles may become important as screening mechanisms, although there are many questions about how to develop efficient but flexible profiles or software "intelligent agents." There are varieties of narrowness and broadness required for information searches, and all points on the specificity continuum must be accommodated. Sometimes the filter should be highly focused on a specific topic. At other times the user wants to see a broad range of articles that are significant and new in a field. In large fields such as molecular biology, the

---

[24]See note 19, *supra*.

[25]See, for example, TULIP experiments undertaken by Elsevier in conjunction with several universities and the "Red Sage" project at the University of California, San Francisco involving Springer-Verlag as well as others.

degree of specialization in the field and the large number of publications may demand a finer filter than a field such as ancient Egyptian literature and linguistics.

Information filtering and selection also create technological demands to improve all-inclusive search mechanisms, with which a scholar can "surf" through information using hypertext. Generally, the technology to enable librarians to develop a new generation of information searching functions is young, but the added value of the activity can only increase in the digital environment.

Technological change is also occurring in the design of information materials. The widespread use of personal computers has made everyone a potential book designer. The need for, and added value of, effective visual design increases in multimedia, which is richer, contains more content, references more widely, and may involve not just illustrations but moving pictures and music or other sound. Applications of multimedia technology to scholarly and professional information have begun — for example, with the ADAM anatomy CD-ROM for medical students or medical continuing education CD-ROMs to teach surgeons new procedures. These sorts of projects require high skill levels among designers and programmers. On the other hand, much of the information sent over the Internet has devalued the design function in order to use the universal ASCII transmission format. Users may impose their own visual designs on incoming electronic signals if a journal, for example, is available only on line or via a local area network. That should lead to a need for upgrading equipment and increasing speed on networks to facilitate design functions. Or users may need to decide to what extent they value good design. They also benefit from electronic data base technology because it reduces user error rates. Spelling and the accuracy of text references, for example, are easily checked when the entire work of an author is on CD-ROM.

We are already seeing marked change in printing and production functions. New technology allows publishers, librarians and end users to "print on demand." New photocopying technology such as DocuTech increases the ability to anthologize and adapt data for a variety of uses and users, and to print small numbers of copies economically. These new opportunities enhance, rather than replace, traditional printed product. Few participants in the information cycle expect print information to disappear.

Intellectual changes

Significant change is occurring as new information communities are created. Scholars perform peer review through use of and commentary on what is on line; the "invisible college" has evolved into new "virtual" clusters of researchers, writers and observers who transcend disciplinary and institutional changes. Librarians will bring people together with information in an integrated system of text and image data bases, and provide them with online tools to build, maintain and share databases. Librarians are developing new collaborative roles with faculty. The interpretive, evaluative and guidance skills of library professionals will therefore continue to be highly valued in the electronic age.

Electronic access to and delivery of information can create a whole new interpretation of "one stop shopping," where the one stop is a scholar's workstation, and the library is virtual rather than locative. This is at the far end of the scale of library decentralization, and has engendered discussion on some campuses about how the library or the university computer center should relate in controlling the menu, defining the structure and acting as gatekeeper of electronic information.

The added value of libraries' reference and cataloging functions will become more important in a world of electronic publishing, though the form will change as libraries become partners with information management systems. Much of the work which librarians do in the area of reference and guidance, however, will be free of the physical constraints of the library. We are not yet able to see clearly how this freedom from physically defined territories and objects will play itself out.

Librarians are challenged by electronic publishing just as surely as publishers. Libraries have become the largest customer of indexing and abstracting services, not actually owning collections but using cataloging, abstracting and indexing services to permit patrons to select required materials.

Finally, librarians add value to the scholarly communication process by preserving culture and assuring democratic access to our shared history through archiving and indexing. We may be moving toward an electronic Alexandria-- a multi-cited, computer accessible repository of all that is best in the world's civilization.

THREE SCENARIOS FOR AN ELECTRONIC FUTURE: CHALLENGES AND OPPORTUNITIES FOR PUBLISHERS AND LIBRARIANS IN THE ELECTRONIC ENVIRONMENT

The Joint Working Group looked at the possible outcomes of different levels of collaboration between publishers and librarians in the rapidly changing technological environment, and looked at the benefits and problems associated with the projected outcomes. While collaboration can occur to various degrees, and outcomes are never assured, three competing scenarios were selected that characterized the range of possibilities: the Null Scenario, the Enlightened Self-Interest Scenario and the Breakthrough Scenario. Figure 4 depicts the framework used to generate the scenarios. It positions current patterns in the ways publishers and librarians collaborate with that of each of the three new scenarios in the framework.

Figure 4.
Framework for Scenario Development

| | | Amount of Change | | |
		Low	Medium	High
Collaboration	Low	Status Quo (Not realistic)	Null or Bypass	
	Medium		Enlightened Self-Interest	
	High			Breakthrough

This framework is based on the publishers' and librarians' perspective (in terms of the degree of "change" to the value-added processes they each perform). Of equal importance is the impact on the users and the authors (often the same individuals) of scholarly journals. Here we assume that "amount of change" in the medium or high range will benefit the user as well, in terms of increased speed, and/or ease of access and possible reduced cost.

In all cases the environment is assumed to be one consisting of networked, on-line information. CD-ROMs, for example, were considered of marginal use, something of a "transitional technology," in the view of librarians. There are scenario-specific assumptions spelled out in each written description.

In addition, each scenario is also characterized by Players and Processes as well as Advantages and Disadvantages. Finally, each scenario dramatizes how the world would look if this scenario were a reality.

The Null Scenario

Assumptions: The environment is fully networked. Only information in electronic form is considered "available." Publishers no longer exist in their current guise. Libraries have also been bypassed. Value-added functions had been provided by both publishers and librarians, but both groups were overcome by self-publishing and Internet distribution. Some value-added functions are traded off in exchange for eliminating the bottlenecks around timelines and affordability. New mechanisms for delivery of information now dominate. Interfaces for end-user access such as NCSA Mosaic and its successors provide the navigating and screening processes, and users extract and input material they wish to use without formal "publication."

Players: Software developers, network operators and scholars make up the players in this scenario. Whatever quality control exists is done via peer review and peer pressure (with occasional intervention by network operators when material "hogs" resources).

Processes: Authors write and review as well as read. They negotiate fees, where appropriate, with networks (or nodes on a network). Networks provide document production processes, archiving, and cost recovery mechanisms. Software developers produce tools for automatic cataloging, navigation/mapping/linking and usage tracking, and provide these tools free or for a fee to network operators.

The World in the Null Scenario: The world is chaotic but exciting. There is very little control regarding what resides on the "net," and explorers discover gems as well as large quantities of useless information. Entrepreneurs who advertise their wares on the net are plentiful. These wares include offers of help in finding needed information. These are mostly the more aggressive librarian-trained individuals seeking new work. Their counterparts in publishing, e.g. editors, also offer their services on the net, but with less success.

Advantages of the Null Scenario:
More timely information.
Easier feedback (via linked commentary).
More convenient access.
Local copying on demand.
Potential for creative use of hypertext links and multi-media features.
Instant "publication" (with little rejection).
Lower apparent cost to universities.
Incentive to develop new network tools.
Costs appear to decline (see below).

Disadvantages of the Null Scenario:
Lack of screening or validation.
Lack of quality control and editing standards.
Lack of preservation of a fixed copy (for the record and for duplicating
    scientific research).
Lack of preservation of "best in class."
Difficulty in knowing and locating everything that is available, and
    differentiating valuable from useless information.
Unclear how copyright could be implemented.
Job loss for publishers and librarians.
Costs are spread and many become hidden.

Dramatization: Neither publishers nor librarians exist in this new academic environment. Instead, Professor Adler uses one of the ubiquitous authoring and indexing software tools on his word processor to prepare his article on previously unidentified rhetorical devices as revealed by new translations of ancient Greek political discourse and the constitutions of the 158 ancient Greek states. He organizes a Mosaic-like document with easy hypertext links. Finished by two o'clock, by two thirty he has notified his friends and colleagues that it is available by putting it on an Internet listserver. Adler is pleased that "publication" has occurred without the old delays, rejections and revisions demanded by the print process. His control over his article to this point has been complete.

Although in the past he has not charged for the works he has self-published on the Internet, he decides to charge for his new effort because he wants to recover some of his costs. In addition to buying software, he has negotiated licenses with Harvard and Oxford University to include the classics data bases, formerly published by their now defunct Presses, in his multi-media Windows-based system. To charge, he needs to be able to collect, so he has spent a tedious amount of time with his bank negotiating access to their Internet-based cash transaction system, paying a fee to Visa to collect payment.

Assistant Professor Warrington met Adler at a scholarly meeting last summer. She is interested in his work on ancient Greek philology, and regularly scans her listserver for his new articles. The abstract looks interesting, so she enters her credit card number, downloads the article on her computer and prints out one copy to read over a cup of coffee at Starbuck's II. She takes exception to Adler's interpretations of Pisistratus' role in conserving the Solonian constitution and reforming Delos as the center of Ionian religion. She herself has put articles on these topics on the Internet, although her only response came from a graduate student in Romania. She is concerned that her Chairwoman will not accept the Romanian commentary as support for her tenure application. So on returning to her office she calls up Adler's Internet address, accesses his working file and corrects the "mistakes" in his article and adds commentary, referring to her Internet contributions.

The first print-out is hard to read. It has come without margins and pagination and the text is in ASCII, so she spends several hours designing a document on her own computer that she can print out and take to Kinko's to make twenty copies for her class in Anthropology 115: Religion and State in the Ancient World (without paying royalties to Adler).

Professor Drang, a political scientist, does not know Adler, but he is working at home on his own article on antecedents of the modern Greek parliament. His need to get information on the primary sources in classical Greek has motivated him to learn how to develop, adapt and use others' subject-specific pointing and search tools to locate new articles. For his own paper, he needs to incorporate information on Solon's democratization of the Areopagus. The title and abstract of Professor Adler's article come up in his search, and he adds the citation to his bibliography, although he can't make out what Adler means in his third paragraph. The good thing is that he can refer to the full Loeb Classical Library edition of Aristotle's *Athenaion Politeia* and *The Oxford Classical Dictionary* on Windows as he reads the confusing parts.

Associate Professor Girardot roomed with Adler in graduate school, but he hasn't checked his e-mail in three weeks because of information overload, and he is considering removing his name from all but one of the Internet listserv groups.

Ms. Burkhardt, a graduate student, searches for Internet contributions by her teachers, but misses Adler's piece because of her inexperience in designing search parameters. The rather acid comments of Professor Beyer, her advisor, as to the depth of her literature search set her dissertation proposal back six months. She looks for professional advice on creating enduser pointing tools and takes another part-time waitressing job to pay a freelance researcher (a former librarian) to do a mediated literature search. She wishes someone would just guide her to what is worth reading.

Jane Torrance, University Comptroller at Warrington's institution, is pleased that rationing faculty electricity and telephone usage to two and a half hours a day and substituting teaching assistants for three lectureship positions in the Classics Department have resulted in sufficient savings to pay the interest on the loan to buy their computers and also make a small contribution to the development costs of the Consortium of University Standard Interactive Networks. Meanwhile the Academic Dean, not conversant in ancient Greek, sets aside a certain tenure review, and wishes there were an objective outsider to place or withhold an imprimatur on Warrington's work.

Six months later, Adler is asked at the last possible moment to present a paper at a convocation in Russia. Remembering his philological piece on Greek rhetorical devices and the Athenian and other constitutions — and thinking of some ironic asides on the present level of debate in the modern Russian Parliament — as he is about to dash for his plane he copies the article onto a floppy disk to revise on the way to St. Petersburg. Unfortunately, much of what he originally wrote has been changed by Ms. Warrington and others, the new material is unfamiliar, and he is tired of getting e-commentaries from that student in Romania, who only wants a sponsor, a visa and a teaching position in America. He remembers that he had gotten some permissions requests for multiple copies of the article, but he wasn't sure of how reprint permissions worked with the licenses from Harvard and Oxford and was too busy find out, so the requests have remained in his in-basket. He is last seen using his modem in the Frankfurt transit lounge trying to retrieve other, earlier self-publications to present to the Russian convocation.

Meanwhile a young scholar in Japan is trying to develop an annotated bibliography of information on ancient Greek philology, but his "tight" searches on the network for English-language scholarship provide few citations, and his "broad" searches keep coming up with strange bits about speeches by politicians and priests. Nothing he tries provides a sufficient selection for his bibliography, and he concludes that western scholarship is worthless.

The Enlightened Self-Interest Scenario

Assumptions: The enlightened self-interest scenario preserves roles for publishing houses, libraries and computer centers in the traditional sense. The process of getting work "into print" does not change, even with the electronic journal. The world is not yet fully networked. Most publications still appear in print, with a slow migration toward electronic publication by commercial publishers and a more rapid migration to the electronic form by not-for-profit publishers and self-publishers. As yet, few people are making money over the network; still, user friendly interfaces, searching tools, encryption and authentication technology are all developing rapidly. The roles of publisher and library remain similar to the present but begin to evolve into a collaborative partnership, motivated both by new technology and by the demand for change from the constituencies of both libraries and publishers. The formerly distinct roles of library and computer center are merging as technology becomes as important as collection development.

Players: Publishers (commercial, non-for-profit) continue to identify and seek out good scholarship and assure that material is peer reviewed before publication. Publishers' methods of operation change as they begin to invest in producing their material in digital form, so that they can provide material over networks, in print, on CD-ROM, or in hand-held computer form. Authors submit work to book and journal publishers as they do now. Libraries (including computer centers) continue their role in collection development, cataloging, storing and archiving material. Libraries' methods of operation change as they begin to develop large scale data storage capability. Innovative technology companies develop large scale networks and large scale data storage capabilities for both libraries and publishers. University computer centers continue to provide automated processes including database management and networking.

Processes: The traditional role of each player is unchanged. Collaboration proceeds in a turf- and tradition-bound sense. Processes such as product development within the publishing houses and collection development and management within libraries remain similar to the present but are much more automated and initially require large amounts of funding. However, many experiments between publishers and libraries spring up. Both groups collaborate on developing compatible networks and data storage for transfer of material from publisher to library, thus easing initial technology investment for both. Technology companies develop systems to automate cataloging, provide searching and navigation tools, and capabilities to track usage and fees. Experiments between publishers and universities or other players proceed in a bilateral manner with little exchange of information across broader boundaries where overall radical change can occur.

The World in the Enlightened Self-interest Scenario: There is little or no change for the author relative to the traditional information flow. For the information user (who may also be an author), access to information may occur via an online network, but the underlying processes remain unchanged with traditional publishing serving a quality control function, and library systems providing the organized access mechanisms to material once it is published. Enlightened libraries have developed integrated databases of full text, image and video files, and enlightened publishers have joined libraries in the development of compatible electronic delivery systems. Publishers are experimenting with various delivery and payment schemes to libraries, e. g. tape transfers plus print at reduced prices; network licenses; licenses to hotlink to the publisher's Internet node or to pay-as-you-go upon entering the node. This is a period when there is much experimentation with format, payment schemes and technology development. It is a truly transitional period for both publisher and library.

> *Advantages of the Enlightened Self-interest Scenario*:
> Current players continue to serve user needs as they see them.
> Current users continue to use service providers they understand.
> Current users begin to receive the information in the way they want, as several kinds of formats exist.

Current players have an opportunity to explore economic and user issues in a less hostile environment.
Pilot projects already underway support this approach.

Disadvantages of the Enlightened Self-interest Scenario:

Projects may not apply to all types and sizes of libraries (and therefore to all users).

Projects can be fragmented and results may not transfer. Process improvements will not provide for fundamental change because of the traditional view of players' roles.

Protection of intellectual property remains an issue; encryption technology not yet foolproof.

Electronic downstreaming further jeopardizes publishers' income.

The successful economic model for publishers has not yet been proved out and risk could be great.

The library could disappear if publishers decide to deal directly with the library constituency.

Dramatization: Professor Smith recently purchased a "high end" workstation which has been configured to meet her own research and teaching needs. She decided to invest some of her faculty development funds in new equipment and software, rather than spending it on professional travel, because she discovered that she is using networked information more frequently. Her library and computer center have now merged and provide excellent training courses on creating effective search techniques and Internet navigation using Mosaic and Gopher, among others. She has become involved in many listserves with colleagues around the world. She has also noticed that she seldom visits the library's physical location, since so many of the library materials she needs are in a digital form which can easily be searched. Materials from many publishers are linked, so she can move easily between articles or chapters regardless of source.

Some of the networked information she uses has been acquired by the university library and she finds it catalogued in the library's online catalogue. Professor Smith also finds a great deal of information on the Internet. Some of her colleagues spend even more time than she on the Internet, participating in various discussion groups and exchanging drafts of papers. She thought that her new equipment would save her time because she could use such tools as Mosaic and WWW more easily, but she worries about "information overload."

Professor Smith has learned from the head librarian, Mrs. Green, that the library is covering the cost of the networked materials from different publishers. The library/computer center is examining user behavior and usage levels to determine future economic models. Mrs. Green has also told her about the various experiments in licensing fees with a myriad of publishers and complains about how complicated it has become. Mrs. Green is thinking about limiting the usage by students, as they seem to be the most frequent users and spend hours navigating around the library network (as well as the Internet), seemingly without scholarly purpose, according to her. Professor Smith begins to worry that she will have to use more of her own grant money for materials if the library decides on an economic model that charges customers. On the other hand, she is pleased that the university has decided to upgrade some of its classrooms with equipment that makes it easier for her to use in her lectures the information resources that have been acquired by the library and made available on the network. She also appreciates the more efficient services provided by the merged library and computer center, whose formerly separate staffs now seem to be working much more closely together.

Of course, Professor Smith does not find everything she needs for her scholarly work in her own library or on the Internet, but Ted Lee, the library bibliographer assigned to her department, is helpful in offering leads to alternate sources. When an article or book is not available locally or cannot be downloaded, he suggests a choice of delivery options ranging from the traditional Interlibrary Loan to a very rapid commercial service. If she chooses the more rapid service, she pays for it. When her faculty development fund runs out, she uses her own credit card to pay.

Many students own personal computers, but Ann Jones, a first year student in Professor Smith's course, decided not to buy one. Instead, she uses computers available in libraries and computer labs to do the assignments for Professor Smith's class. Ann also spends a good deal of time in the library's new electronic reserve room, where Professor Smith has made additional materials available. Ann may buy her own computer next year because she would be able to do the reserve readings and course assignments from her dorm room. Of course, she would still go to the library. The library has material that is not available on the network, and it is the place on campus to meet people and to study with friends.

Ted recently invited Professor Smith and her class, including Ann, to participate in a pilot project that the library and computer center are undertaking. Ted is co-chair of the task force for this project, one of several that are taking place on the campus. The library has developed agreements with several publishers to make their currently produced material available in digital form on the campus network. Professor Smith and Ann Jones have each been asked to fill out questionnaires and have agreed to be interviewed about their use of the information. Other aspects of the project involve studying the costs to the library, to the computer center and to the publishers. Two of the information providers involved in the pilot project are Dr. Brown and Mr. Black.

Dr. Brown is a prominent author who has worked for years with several publishers. He finally decided to start his own electronic journal and has made it available on the library network. At the same time, he has been approached by a commercial publisher to produce an electronic subscription project. Since the publisher is willing to provide all the funding for equipment and secretarial help, as well as a model for a completely electronic editorial office, he has decided to join forces with the publisher.

Mr. Black, an executive at one of the leading medical publishing houses, has directed his company's heavy investment in electronic delivery systems with libraries. He has also taken the lead in moving his publishing house toward electronic product development. He knows it is a risk, but he also knows that hesitation in moving from paper to electronics will put him far behind his competition, if not out of business. Still, he worries about the level of capital investment required, and he worries as well about the protection of copyrights his company holds. His counterpart at the university press says many of the same things. It surprises Professor Smith and Ted Lee that the commercial publisher and the university press seem to have such similar points of view, since they have heard about the difference between the "commercial" and the "not-for-profit" publishers.

They all agree at one of their frequent project meetings that this is a time when they are discovering more about their own operations, about the use of information by faculty and students, and about each other.

Sometimes Ted has a difficult time keeping up with the many projects taking place on the campus. It seems to him that for a long time publishers, computer center staff and librarians were suspicious or even hostile toward one another. Now it seems that he hears about similar projects taking place at many universities. Ted wonders if these projects will really lead to the significant changes he reads about. His own budget for acquisitions has not increased enough to keep pace with the increases in the costs of information. He knows that Jean Rowan, the computer center staffer who is co-chairing the task force with him, wonders whether the university administration will be able to continue to fund the upgrade of the campus network and the additional hardware and software necessary to keep pace with all of the digital information. She says her colleagues at the computer center are feeling as stretched as the librarians in their efforts to keep pace with new developments and to continue to deliver the services that the faculty and students have come to expect.

The Breakthrough Scenario

Assumptions: The environment is fully networked with virtually all information (or at least surrogates of information such as summaries or bibliographic descriptions) existing in electronic form, regardless of its original form of publication. The access mechanisms available to users are barrier free and as easy to use as current voice communications systems such as the telephone. Boundaries between different players in the delivery process are dissolving, and the focus is on improving the processes as opposed to defending the territories of the current players.

Players: In addition to the libraries and the publishers, other players include authors, users and emerging non-traditional competitors in the information arena (e.g., independent information brokers). Old ways of thinking built "chimneys" or barriers around each of these players.

Processes: Activities include the authoring processes, archiving and cataloging, navigating/ mapping/linking of information, quality and authentication functions and methods of cost recovery. For breakthroughs to occur, players must focus on process improvement and redesign, not protection of old methods or territories.

The World in the Breakthrough Scenario: The world initially looks very much like that in the Null Scenario. There is a period of considerable disorientation as organizations give up their old ways of thinking of themselves and how they bring value to the users. The system of scholarly communication may actually regress temporarily as players try to determine survival strategies. During this period some organizations representing certain players may disappear. Some libraries may close (such as the Engineering Societies Library that recently closed in New York City), some publishers may go out of business. In the long run, however, if the players mutually discover that survival depends on better services to their customers, they will collaborate in creating totally new ways of getting the job done. As an example, many libraries would like to outsource cataloging to a service provider that would imbed it in the acquisition process.

> *Advantages of the Breakthrough Scenario*:
>> Increased business opportunities for current and new players.
>> Old assumptions get rethought.
>> Improved flow of information and the workflow supporting the process.
>> Functions are retained based on benefit to the user rather than on the current market value.

> *Disadvantages of the Breakthrough Scenario*:
>> Period of disruption precedes breakthrough.
>> Traditional roles disappear.
>> Cost of transition is on top of current costs, and includes retraining costs.
>> Job loss for publishers and librarians.
>> Potential loss of real benefits that are not readily seen by users/players, although this would be corrected in the long run.
>> Resource sharing (a traditional library function) may not be maintained.

Dramatization: After a period of delight with the speed of the Global Information Infrastructure (GII, offspring of the Internet), Caroline Leary, an associate professor at a major midwestern research university, has become disenchanted. She and some of her colleagues meet with the campus library director to see if he can help them with their complaints, which include:

> Lack of a systematic way to locate (and place) information in the national network;
> Multiple lists, servers, gophers and other sources providing similar, but often contradictory, information and citations to sources that cannot be found, or when found exist in various versions, none of which can be authenticated;
> Increasing difficulty in printing hard copies of material in a format that is suitable for further distribution because of the variety of techniques by which material is being submitted into the system;
> Continued difficulty in obtaining permission to reproduce material for course distribution, because of the widely varying distribution restrictions on material provided on the network.

As a result of this initial meeting and several subsequent ones, the faculty and library management meet with a group of publishers to discuss a "whole systems approach" to the scholarly communication processes. At the same time, they begin discussing these same issues at their professional society meetings and enlist support from other institutions. The university faculty, while not driven by cost factors, is concerned by what it sees as diminished support for information services at a time when faculty members are being told they are in the "information age."

Their university administration, initially concerned only with reducing the cost of library operations, now begins to look at the total cost of the scholarly communication processes in place. They soon recognize that the library budget is only a small part of the university investment in these activities, and that overall inefficiency is far more costly than library journal prices. As an example, the time faculty spend in identifying and finding relevant information (including putting together course material) is the largest cost item related to information processing on campus. The administrative leadership, too, becomes interested in working with any organization that could help reduce costs. They see publishers (and other organizations) as potential allies in their initiative to contain costs.

Carolyn Leary agrees to lead a faculty task force to explore new ways to produce scholarly information and distribute it to colleagues on other campuses. She insists that the task force include a library representative as well as representatives from commercial and not-for-profit publishing and their own university's press. She soon finds that similar task forces exist on other campuses and suggests that a conference be held to bring these people together for an open discussion of the issues. As a result, a formalized network of scholars across several disciplines is established to begin to coordinate the development of electronic scholarly journals. Professional societies, major players in the not-for-profit publishing arena, at first resist, but ultimately join the networking effort, once they realize their own members are moving ahead of them.

In the following year many small breakthroughs occur. The director of the library, Frank Grim, working with a group of his peers and a group of publishers, begins to take on a prospecting function for publishers, by identifying potential authors of manuscripts on emerging areas of scholarly interest. The library is a logical place to put this function, he believes, since librarians often hear of emerging areas very early. In addition, the library becomes the one-stop location for copyright clearance on material for course packs.

Grim also announces that the library will no longer catalogue the material it purchases. Instead, it will work with outside vendors to purchase "standard cataloging records." Projected savings are to be invested in the purchase of additional access rights to some of the emerging electronic services and publications. Equally important, the cataloging backlog is being eliminated, and with this new approach will cease to be a major problem.

Several publishers begin getting in touch with several key library facilities, including Grim's, to discuss archiving the emerging electronically "published" material. The understanding is that the library will preserve the material in a retrievable form. In addition, the designated library facilities, such as Grim's, will track the usage of such material and report demand to publishers for copyright and prospecting purposes.

Material entered in the electronic network now can now be tagged as informal communication, preprint material, published material, or out-of-print but archived material; that is, it is no longer current enough to be stored for immediate access in on-line facilities, but it will still be available upon request in electronic form. Informal communication is still a private matter between participants and does not directly contribute to the scholarly reward system. Preprints — formal distribution of material prior to peer review and publication — are enhanced by the electronic network, but controlled so that authors and publishers can still benefit from the formal publication process. Once formally published, the material is tagged, provided with an electronic "watermark" and indexed in secondary publication products, and also, by peer review, acknowledged as to its acceptance.

Publishers, working with such faculty networks as the one started by Carolyn, begin to assemble a suite of software packages for authors to use in organizing their material for electronic publication. In addition, publishers work with libraries to provide an organizational structure to preprint and published material. This structure begins to "trickle down" to the informal material as well, and some of the problems that prompted Carolyn's initial interest begin to be resolved.

While breakthroughs are not rapid, when they occur they invariably redistribute functions and eliminate old bottlenecks. The partnerships and alliances created by faculty, administration and outside vendors lead to additional breakthroughs that cannot even be imagined here.

CONCLUSIONS, RECOMMENDATIONS, AND NEXT STEPS

The most beneficial outcome of the Joint Working Group's efforts was to build a shared knowledge base and understanding of the roles, functions and added value provided by publishers and librarians both currently and in the electronic future. This allowed the Group to identify and address many of the bottlenecks that challenge publishers and librarians to operate effectively in the new electronic environment.

If publishers and librarians have, until now, imperfectly understood what the others do and how value is added to information as it moves through organizations, then the other players in the scholarly communication process are even less likely to have a clear idea about these contributions. This would include authors, university faculty members and administrative staff, researchers, students, electronic experts such as programmers at university computer centers, participants in the distribution process and end users of all types. Many of these players are currently involved in rethinking how scholarship is and will be disseminated.

> *Recommendation:* It was the view of members of the Joint Working Group that every effort should be made to communicate the results of its work to all participants in the scholarly information process. In its following recommendations, the Group brings a variety of potential projects to the attention of the sponsoring organizations and all those to whom this report is communicated, with a view toward influencing such groups to pursue and support such projects.

The value added concept implies a confirmation by end users that the contributions do, indeed, have value. In market terms this confirmation is usually provided by the end users' willingness to purchase the product or service at a price perceived as reasonable in relation to the value supplied. Yet little has been done to date on end users' awareness or validation of purchasers' and librarians' value added.

> *Recommendation:* Create an end user survey and/or focus groups to test and increase awareness and to validate, reexamine or eliminate value added functions in the electronic environment.

A number of collaborative efforts are underway to explore new ways of disseminating scholarly information, many of which are listed in Appendix E (p. 65). There has been to date no systematic way of keeping track of what pilot projects are underway, being conducted by whom to reach

what goals. At the same time, various groups are attempting to develop model licensing agreements

that account for ownership, archiving (and allowing revision while preserving an original work),

resource sharing, fees based on capitation (as in the medical model of HMO's or the Copyright

Clearance Center's work on university member capitation-based licensing), licensing electronic tapes

for LAN and WAN dissemination through university-based interfaces and transaction-based fees

paid by users, among many others.

> *Recommendation*: The Joint Working Group supports the expansion of pilot projects
> to track / influence information access, usage and distribution processes, and the
> design of new models. The Group recommends the development of a Clearinghouse
> of projects currently underway. At the simplest level, a base of information could be
> gathered by asking members of the Group and its sponsoring organizations to list
> all projects known to each. Alternatively, a study could be commissioned by the
> sponsoring organizations to be followed by a distributed, on-line, updatable report on
> Internet.

Further research and analysis are needed on the economics of library functions (e.g.,

technical services, archiving, cataloging) and publishing costs. The goal would be to create baseline

economic models for both groups by which to evaluate the economic impact of eliminating or

changing functions. This work can build on projects already underway, including those currently

conducted by the Coalition for Networked Information (CNI) and Rutgers University through

funding from the Council on Library Resources. Results of these and other projects can help pro-

mote greater understanding of the economic impact of various strategies for change. For example,

we have seen that a monograph publisher who used new technologies to achieve a 10% savings in

production costs would reduce overall costs by only 3%. We have also seen that library technical

services account for something less than half of total costs, but analytical tools do not yet exist for

evaluating what could be saved by shifting or outsourcing the cataloging function in academic

libraries.

> *Recommendation*: Design and fund a project to establish baseline models of
> functions, services and cost by function (as was done in the Research Libraries
> Group/Association of Research Libraries' Inter-Library Loan cost analysis, funded
> by the Council on Library Resources), and to create analytical tools for evaluating
> the impact of eliminating, shifting or outsourcing specific functions and/or services.
> Such a project should involve as many stakeholders as possible, in order to create a
> model of the economics of the information publishing and dissemination process.

Archiving has been a traditional function and added value of libraries, but it has also been the source of high costs for shelf space, physical plant, preservation technology development and applications. The complexity of archiving increases as electronically stored materials become "unreadable" without the preservation of related software, and as the materials of electronic publishing such as CD-ROM and floppy disks age. For example, current CD-ROMs last only 50 years, and today's machines that "read" electronic products will be soon be obsolete.

> *Recommendation*: Work with organizations having an interest in preservation (e.g. The Association of Research Libraries, the Commission on Preservation and Access, and the Library of Congress) to design and seek funding for an archiving issues project to develop policies and assign related responsibilities. The project would investigate how to create permanent archives given the continually changing technology. Questions to be reexamined would include: *Who* should archive? *Where? What* should be archived? *How* will the archives be protected from unauthorized scanning and on-demand printing?

There is a perception among librarians and publishers that the electronic revolution is changing the way scholarship is disseminated more rapidly than at any other time, perhaps since the invention of movable type. This is both exciting and frightening to participants in the information process. There is a need for participants to identify where opportunities lie in the new environment, in order for the "electronic revolution" to have positive results.

> *Recommendation*: A study designed to identify "windows of opportunity" and thereby prioritize actions should be conducted. One appropriate methodology for such a project would be the "Delphi" technique, in which several experts estimate how fast specific changes might occur, and then group consensus is sought through a series of feedback cycles and revised estimates.[26] These predictions could then be used to provide guidelines on how much time publishers, librarians, and other stakeholders might have to act or react. See, for example, the study done by F. W. Lancaster on the impact of technological change on the future of libraries.[27]

Libraries have traditionally been the repository of much published work that is "out of print" or no longer available from the originating publisher. If publishers' out-of-print archives were made

---

[26]Harold A. Linstone and Murray Turoff (editors), *The Delphi Method - Techniques and Applications*, Reading, MA: Addison-Wesley Publishing Co. (1975).

[27]F. W. Lancaster, "The Impact of a Paperless Society on the Research Library of the Future," a report to the National Science Foundation by the Library Research Center, University of Illinois (1980). Available from NTIS as PB 80-204548.

available through libraries electronically, and printed on demand, would usage of this information increase? Could publishers be paid for such use?

> *Recommendation*: Design and fund a project to research the effect of electronic announcement, ordering or transmission/display on useful life of documents. This project could be designed around data already available on document requests before and after various changes in access mechanisms to test the assumption that expanding or simplifying identification, ordering and delivery of various types of documents will increase their useful life (and demand for them over time).

Finally, members of the Joint Working Group on Professional and Scholarly Information in the Electronic Age perceived their participation as beneficial. Their shared information and understanding could form the basis for further collaborative investigation and negotiation of points of controversy, common research needs, operational advances, functional shifts and policy development. The Joint Working Group was designed for just two of the stakeholders in the scholarly information process. Its members were well aware that other stakeholders need to be involved in designing effective responses to the opportunities and challenges of the electronic revolution.

> *Recommendation*: Support the formation of other similar groups that include other stakeholders, such as authors, end users, distributors, agencies and information services, secondary publishers, and copyright and permissions professionals. Draw on the Joint Working Group's experience and shared base of information and understanding by "seeding" new groups with Joint Working Group members. Such groups or task forces could be organized around some of the specific issues and areas for research raised in this Report, or in relation to other timely issues that arise from the development of a national information infrastructure.

For further information on these recommendations and how to participate in their implementation, contact:

Professional/Scholarly Publishing Division
Association of American Publishers, Inc.
71 Fifth Avenue
New York, NY 10003
Tel: (212) 255-0200
Fax: (212) 255-7007
email: bjmeredith@mcimail.com

Council on Library Resources
1400 16th Street, NW
Suite 510
Washington, DC 20036
Tel: (202) 483-7474
Fax: (202) 483-6410
email: clr@cni.org

APPENDIX A

Project Description

The following Project Description was circulated to and approved by the two sponsoring

organizations in September, 1993:

> Objective: To bring publishers and librarians together to address common issues of value added contributions in the emerging electronic environment.
>
> Sponsors: Council on Library Resources and the Professional/Scholarly Publishing Division, Association of American Publishers, Inc.
>
> Participants: Seven librarians and seven professional and scholarly publishers [see Appendix B].
>
> Format: At least three meetings, to take place in New York in November 1993, Washington in February 1994 and Chicago in May 1994, with a deadline of completing the work described below by June 1994.
>
> Agenda:
> Identify the value added by librarians and publishers in the electronic information environment.
> Define roles of the publisher and the librarian when information is delivered directly to the academic or researcher's desk/PC.
> Address the "bottlenecks" and opportunities that challenge librarians and publishers to operate effectively in the new environment, e.g., demand for immediate, high quality, low cost information that is quickly and easily accessed and, often, manipulated and/or printed at the scholar's or researcher's desk.
> Explore how new alliances could be designed to enhance publishers' and librarians' roles and added value to the scholarly and research process.
> Relate intellectual property rights to the ideas addressed above.
>
> Facilitator: Select a neutral (i.e., identified with neither the publishing nor the librarian communities) research firm to aid discussion within the Working Group and to facilitate research into roles and added values and document results.
>
> Funding: Costs to be shared equally by the sponsors, not to exceed a total budget of $15,000, to cover the costs of the facilitator, meeting sites and travel costs for selected participants.
>
> Outcome: Develop a plan for librarians and publishers to promote new concepts and alliances to academic and research communities. Increase understanding of how publisher and librarian roles and added value change when scholarship and information is transmitted electronically. Identify possible new alliances based on the research and dialogue produced by the Joint Working Group. Develop a plan to disseminate the results.

APPENDIX B

Participants

Seven library representatives and seven publishing representatives were chosen on the basis of their interest in the topic, the respect they held among their peers, and their ability to focus, decide and delegate to advance the process. The co-sponsors hired a consultant to help design and facilitate the Joint Working Group's progress. A preliminary statement of contributions and concerns of each group was prepared, and participants were asked to give the matter their consideration before the series of meetings began. Participants included:

Janet D. Bailey, Group Publisher, Elsevier Science Inc.

Janet D. Bailey is responsible for managing the medical journals program at Elsevier, as well as advertising sales and rights and permissions. Prior to coming to Elsevier in 1985, she was Vice President at Knowledge Industry Publications, Inc., Director of Inventory and Contracts at Macmillan Books Clubs, Inc., and for six years had been editor of the journal, *Special Libraries*, for the Special Libraries Association. Ms. Bailey is a member of the Executive Council of the Professional/Scholarly Publishing Division of AAP, and previously served as Chair of the Journals Committee for PSP. She has written several research reports about various segments of the publishing industry, including electronic publishing. She holds the MBA in finance from Pace University and a BA in English from the University of Delaware.

Betty Bengtson, Director of University Libraries, University of Washington, Seattle

Betty Bengtson has more than 25 years of experience in academic libraries of various sizes. She is especially interested in the effects of networked distribution of information on libraries, the management of libraries in rapidly changing environments, and staff development and retraining for new technology. Ms. Bengston earned her undergraduate degree from Duke University and her master's degrees from Catholic University and the University of Maryland. She has served as President of the OCLC Users Council and chaired the 1992 national conference of the Library and Information Technology Association. She currently serves on the boards of the Commission on Preservation and Access, the Library and Information Technology Association, and the Seminars on Academic Computing. She also chairs the Association of Research Libraries' Preservation of Library Materials Committee.

Harold Billings, Director, General Libraries, The University of Texas at Austin

Harold Billings has been Director of General Libraries since 1977. He has served on the boards of the Association of Research Libraries, the AMIGOS Bibliographic Council, and the Center for Research Libraries, as well as numerous national groups concerned with resource sharing, networking and preservation. Mr. Billings is author or editor of works dealing with contemporary literature and bibliography, as well as articles about library cooperation and the electronic information revolution.

Robert D. Bovenschulte, Vice President for Publishing, *New England Journal of Medicine*, Waltham, MA

Robert D. Bovenschulte has been in publishing for 27 years and has been the publisher of the New England Journal of Medicine since May 1990. His career spans scholarly, professional, trade, college and school segments of the industry. Functionally, his experience lies in sales, marketing, editorial acquisition and development, and general management. Prior to his current position, Mr. Bovenschulte was Vice President and General Manager of Lexington Books, an imprint and division of D.C. Heath and Company. Before that he was Vice President of Books and Collections, a division of UMI. Mr. Bovenschulte served for six years on the Executive Council of the AAP's Professional/ Scholarly Publishing Division, the last two as Chairman, and he is active in the Society for Scholarly Publishing.

Robert T. Grant, President and Chief Executive Officer, CRC Press, Inc.

Robert T. Grant has been with CRC Press — a Times Mirror company that publishes books, journals, newsletters and electronic products in science and technology — since it became a part of the Times Mirror organization in December 1986. He has served as General Manager and is currently the Company's President and Chief Executive Officer. Prior to joining CRC, he was Vice President of Finance and Administration with Year Book Medical Publishers in Chicago, and Division Controller at Graphic Controls Corporation in Buffalo — both Times Mirror companies. Before that, he spent seven years with Price Waterhouse and Co., and is a Certified Public Accountant in the State of New York.

Robert Grant is Chair of the Professional and Scholarly Publishing Division of the American Association of Publishers and a Member of the Group Executive of the International Group of Scientific, Technical and Medical Publishers (STM).

Margaret M. Irwin, Associate Editorial Director of the Scientific, Technical and Medical Group, John Wiley and Sons, New York

Margaret M. Irwin has spent her publishing career in STM publishing, with nearly 22 years at John Wiley and Sons, Inc. in various marketing, editorial and general management capacities. In addition to managing the engineering, physics, mathematics and statistics programs, she has particular responsibility for spearheading and coordinating electronic publishing activities in STM. Another important achievement for her at Wiley was the creation of the Library Advisory Board, now two years old. Ms. Irwin considers her work and contact with the library community essential in helping plan for the future together.

Barbara J. Meredith, Director, Professional/Scholarly and International Divisions of the Association of American Publishers (AAP), New York

Barbara J. Meredith oversees the AAP's trade association activities of companies responsible for publishing the vast majority of materials produced and used by scholars and professionals in science, medicine, technology, business, law and the social and behavioral sciences. These publishers are worldwide disseminators and shapers of scientific research via print and electronic means. In the International arena, Ms. Meredith coordinates educational and publishing programs for publishers on export sales, the selling of English language and translation rights, international publishing and distribution, book fairs and the protection of copyright in international markets.

Carol Hansen Montgomery, Associate Provost and Director, Center for Academic Informatics, Hahnemann University, Philadelphia

Dr. Carol Hansen Montgomery has been active in the information field for over 20 years as an administrator, teacher, researcher and author. She holds a bachelor's degree in chemistry from Bryn Mawr College and a doctorate in information systems from the College of Information Studies, Drexel University. A frequent contributor to the professional literature, she is the co-author of *Online Searching: A Primer*, published by Learned Information, and author of *The Microcomputer User's Guide to Information Online*, published by Hayden Book Company. Dr. Montgomery is currently Associate Provost and Director, Center for Academic Informatics at Hahnemann University. She has held local and national positions in numerous professional organizations including Chair of the Philadelphia Chapter of the Medical Library Association (MLA). She is presently working on MLA's research policy statement as part of a special task force. She has also served on several advisory boards and recently completed a term on the National Library of Medicine's extramural program review committee. She is a member of the OCLC User's Council where she serves on the Resource Sharing Interest Group.

W. David Penniman, President of the Council on Library Resources, Inc., Washington, D.C.

The Council on Library Resources, Inc. is an operating foundation that has been a leader since 1956 in solving problems in information availability. In today's environment, the Council's mission extends to all types of libraries and emerging information services including those that will be carried by the proposed national "information highway." As an operating foundation, the Council performs projects and awards grants and contracts to other organizations to put emerging technologies to use in modern libraries and information systems.

Before joining the Council in 1991, Dr. Penniman served as Director of the Information

Services Group and, prior to that, as Libraries and Information Systems Director at AT&T Bell Laboratories from 1984. He has served as Vice President for Planning and Research for the Online Computer Library Center (OCLC), where he also established the Research Department in 1978. He has worked as a research scholar at the International Institute for Applied Systems Analysis in Austria and as an information scientist at the Battelle Memorial Institute in Columbus, Ohio, where he was also Associate Manager of the Information Systems Section, and managed the group responsible for the development of the BASIS online retrieval and data management system.

Sarah M. Pritchard, Director of Libraries, Smith College, Northampton, MA

Sarah M. Pritchard administers Smith College's library and media services, including collections of over one million items in the William Allan Neilson Library, three branch libraries, and the internationally-known Sophia Smith Collection of women's history manuscripts. Ms. Pritchard holds graduate degrees in French and in Library Science from the University of Wisconsin-Madison. Prior to coming to Smith in 1992, she was the Associate Executive Director at the Association of Research Libraries, responsible for the ARL statistics programs, board and policy coordination, publishing, conference and systems management. From 1977 to 1990, Ms. Pritchard was employed at the Library of Congress in positions related to general reference, microform services, automation and collection development. In 1988-1989, Ms. Pritchard worked at the Princeton University Library as a Council on Library Resources Academic Library Management Intern. An active participant in library and academic associations, she is currently an elected member of the Council of the American Library Association and the board of the New England Chapter of the Association of College and Research Libraries. She has published and lectured widely in the US and abroad on women's studies, automation, collection development, library statistics and other professional issues.

John M. Saylor, Director, Engineering Library, Cornell University

John M. Saylor received his bachelors degree in Materials Science Engineering from the University of Pennsylvania in 1969. He worked for a year as a research engineer at Bethlehem Steel Corporation's Homer Research Laboratory and then returned to academia to pursue a career in information science. He received a Master's of Library Science from Rutgers University in 1971. In 1973 he was hired as the reference librarian in the Engineering Library at Cornell University. In 1987 he became the library director. In 1990 he received funding as CO-Project Investigator for the Standards Study Project associated with the NSF funded engineering education coalition called "Synthesis — A National Engineering Education Coalition." Mr. Saylor has a great interest in the development of the electronic library or "library without walls" concept. He is co-chair of the Cornell Electronic Publishing Working Group, co-editor on the ACRL STS electronic publication called *Issues in Science and Technology Librarianship*, and a member of ASEE, ASIS and ALA.

Linda Scovill, President, Scovill, Paterson Inc., New York

Scovill, Paterson was established in 1990 to publish and disseminate professional information for doctors and student financial aid specialists. Publications include books, newsletters and audiovisual packages. In addition, Scovill, Paterson provides marketing and distribution, publishing and consulting services to societies, institutions and publishers. Prior to starting her own company Ms. Scovill was Vice President, Marketing and Sales of Appleton and Lange, the health sciences division of Simon and Schuster. She had earlier held positions in the International Division of Harper and Row and at both the Oxford and Harvard University Presses. From 1992 - 1994, Linda Scovill chaired the Professional and Scholarly Publishing division of the Association of American Publishers, where her interest in electronic publishing developments and in finding new solutions to resolve conflicts among participants in the information cycle led to the formation of the Joint Working Group.

Robert Shirrell, Journals Manager, University of Chicago Press, Chicago

Robert Shirrell has responsibility for 54 book and journal publications of the University of Chicago Press. He currently serves as president of the Society for Scholarly Publishing. He is a member of the Advisory Committee for Publications of the Art Institute of Chicago, and a member of the Advisory Board of the Publishing Program, Office of Continuing Education at the University of Chicago. He formerly served as chairman of the Scholarly Journals Committee of the Association of American University Presses.

Elaine Sloan, Vice President for Information Services and University Librarian, Columbia University

Elaine Sloan was born in Pittsburgh, Pennsylvania. She received her BA in psychology from Chatham College, MA in history from the University of Pittsburgh, and MLS and PhD in library and information science from the University of Maryland. Before coming to Columbia in 1988, she was Dean of University Libraries at Indiana University, and Associate University Librarian for Public Services at the University of California at Berkeley. At Columbia, she is responsible for the University Libraries and Academic Information Systems. She has been active in the library profession, including serving as President of the Association of Research Libraries in 1988-1989.

Facilitator

Christine Harris, Consultant

Christine Harris has more than ten years' experience as a management consultant focusing on organizational behavior. She brings to the Joint Working Group special skills in facilitating innovative problem-solving sessions, building collaborative work teams and in identifying acceptable solutions to diverse and conflicting interests. Christine completed her undergraduate degree in psychology at Pomona College and is a doctoral candidate in Administration, Planning and Social Policy research at the Harvard Graduate School of Education. Her many clients include AT&T - Bell Laboratories, the Charles River Museum of Industry, Beacon Press and the Engineering Foundation.

APPENDIX C
THE PUBLISHING PROCESS

Marketing	Editorial/Production	Legal/Financial/Operations
Recommend publishing projects based on market trends.	Develop publishing plan.	
Conduct market research. Maintain publisher position.	Review proposal or work quality of sought and/or unsought manuscripts. Solicit peer reviews.	Determine internal/external financing.
	Decide acceptability; select manuscripts for publication.	Conduct financial review.
	Develop and organize content.	Issue author contract; register copyright; assign rights and licenses.
Sell advertising space (journals, optional).	Edit content, language and style, format.	Make financial investment.
Make recommendations and/or approve physical appearance of the publication.	Design physical appearance of the publication.	
Market and Promote design marketing plan, test and implement direct mail, advertise, publicize, promote to subscription agencies and information services (A & I svcs.), send review copies (books), exhibit at scholarly meetings.	Typeset (key), proofread and solicit and make author corrections and revisions. Create pages.	
	Index.	
	Send to printer and binder.	
Sell through telemarketing or field sales force to book stores, wholesalers and libraries worldwide (books). Provide customer services. Sell rights and licenses for dissemination of information in other formats and languages.	Receive and approve finished printed product	Bring into stock. Grant permissions. Track and pay royalties. Enter and fulfill orders. Warehouse. Distribute. Carry out credit and collections.

APPENDIX D

INFORMATION PROCESS IN LIBRARIES

Identification/ Selection	Information Organization	Public Services	Collection Management, etc.
Assess and respond to user needs.	Design access systems. Provide structural information systems. Acquire, order/claim pay.	Provide access to information through interlibrary loan, document delivery, circulation, Selective Dissemination of Information (SDI) and current awareness programs.	Provide housing for collections, shelve and keep in order.
Screen potential purchases.			
Survey, review and synthesize literature for both internal (professional) and external (reader's) use.	Catalogue/Index. Put in local on-line catalogue.	Provide reference and consultation service. Direct people to appropriate sources. Promote and market services.	
Develop intellectually coherent collections.		Subsidize cost of private information.	Archive (long-term).
Develop links to databases and other information providers to provide access to collections not owned locally.	Classify and shelve information.	Instruct/train users.	Develop tools for outside searches.
	Track and analyze overall process.		Decide what to preserve or replace.
	Manage MIS and financial issues.	Provide social, study research environment.	Disseminate collections through campus networks.

APPENDIX E

Selected List of Electronic Projects

Some of the projects discussed:

Online Journal of Current Clinical Trials
> Peer reviewed electronic journal with graphical user interface

American Chemical Society's Chemical Journals Online
> Full-text chemical journals

Postmodern Culture
> Peer-reviewed journal distributed to subscribers through electronic mail

Chemical & Engineering News Online
> Text of scientific magazine articles available electronically

Scientist
> Science newspaper text available online

Public-Access Computer Systems Review
> Online journal table of contents with articles available through ftp

Electronic Text Center, University of Virginia
> Facility designed to bring together online resources of text, reference works, and images to enhance scholarship and teaching

Chemistry Online Retrieval Experiment (CORE)
> Prototype electronic library of journals delivered over local area network (LAN) at Cornell University; partners include Bellcore and OCLC

Red Sage
> Joint venture of University of California—San Francisco, AT&T, and Springer-Verlag to deliver journal images and articles over LAN

TULIP (The University Licensing Program)
> Universities accessing digital collection of Elsevier journal articles utilizing local software

Carnegie Mellon — UMI
> Journal article information stored in jukeboxes for delivery over LAN

McGraw Hill Primus
> System to create customized textbooks

Electronic Chaucer
> Text files linked to color image archives

Electronic Encyclopedia Britannica
> Text to be made available on campus system

APPENDIX F*

Selected Bibliography

Association of American Publishers, Professional/Scholarly Publishing Division's Electronic Information Committee. *Promises & Pitfalls: A Briefing Paper on Internet Publishing.* Czeslaw Jan Grycz, Editor. New York: Association of American Publishers, Inc. (1994).

Association of American University Presses, Scholarly Journals Committee. *1991 Survey of University Press Journals: A Survey of Journals Published by Member and Affiliate Presses of the Association of American University Presses.* New York: Association of American University Presses (1991).

Arnold, Kenneth. "The Scholarly Monograph Is Dead, Long Live the Scholarly Monograph." *Scholarly Publishing on the Electronic Networks...Proceedings of the Second Symposium.* Washington, D. C.: Association of Research Libraries (1993).

Barrett, Jaia; Harvey, Diane; Okerson, Ann and Reed-Scott, Jutta. "AAU Develops a Framework for Change." *ARL (A Bimonthly Newsletter of Research Library Issues and Actions).* No. 170, September, 1993.

Bennett, Scott. "Copyright and Innovation in Electronic Publishing: A Commentary." *Journal of Academic Librarianship.* Volume 19, Number 2, May 1993.

Berry, John N. "New Directions for the Library Lobby." *Library Journal.* Volume 118, Number 9, May 15, 1993.

Billings, Harold. "Supping with the Devil. New Library Alliances in the Information Age." *Wilson Library Bulletin.* October 1993.

Campbell, Robert. "The Commercial Role in Journal Publishing: Past, Present and Future." *Logos.* Vol. 3, No. 1, 1992.

Council on Library Resources. From the President. "Where Does the Money Go (and Where Does It Come From)?" *CLR Reports.* New Series, Number 3, January 1994.

Cox, Meg. "Technology Threatens to Shatter the World of College Textbooks." *Wall Street Journal.* June 1, 1993, p. 1.

Cummings, Anthony M.; Little, Marcia L.; Bowen, William G.; Lazarus, Laura O., and Ekman, Richard H. "University Libraries and Scholarly Communication." A Study Prepared for the Andrew W. Mellon Foundation and published by the Association of Research Libraries (1992).

DeLoughry, Thomas J. "Computers and Copyrights." *Chronicle of Higher Education.* November 24, 1993.

Graham, Gordon. *As I Was Saying.* London: Hans Zell, Publishers (1994).

Guenette, David R. "Publisher's Perspective." *CD ROM World.* February/March, 1993.

---

*This brief bibliography, of course, neither aspires to nor pretends to completeness. It consists of readings used to prepare the matrices for the Joint Working Group, materials suggested from time to time by various members of the Joint Working group, and several items from materials prepared by Julia Blixrud, program officer at the Council on Library Resources.

International Publishers Copyright Council. *The Publisher in the Electronic World: A Discussion Document.* 1993.

Kranich, Nancy C. "Can Libraries Protect Public Access?" *Library Journal.* Volume 118, Number 19, November 15, 1993.

Lancaster, F. W. "The Impact of a Paperless Society on the Research Library of the Future." A Report to the National Science Foundation by the Library Research Center, University of Illinois (1980).

Linstone, Harold A. and Turoff, Murray (editors). *The Delphi Method--Techniques and Applications.* Reading, MA: Addison-Wesley Publishing Co. (1975).

Lucier, Richard E. "Knowledge Management: Refining Roles in Scientific Communication." *EDUCOM Review.* Volume 25, Number 3, Fall 1990.

Maddox, John. "Electronic Journals Are Already Here." *Nature.* Vol. 365, October 21, 1993.

Penniman, W. David. "Visions of the Future: Libraries and Librarianship for the Next Century." The Fifth Nasser Sharif Lecture. New York: Pratt Graduate School of Information and Library Sciences (1993).

Roche, Marilyn M. *ARL/RLG Interlibrary Loan Cost Study--A Joint Effort by the Association of Research Libraries and the Research Libraries Group.* Washington, D.C.: Association of Research Libraries (1993).

Saffo, Paul. "Quality in an Age of Electronic Incunabula." *Liberal Education.* Volume 79, Number 1, Winter 1993.

Sharratt, Bernard. Review of *The Electronic Word: Democracy, Technology and the Arts,* by Richard A. Lanham. *The New York Times Book Review.* November 28, 1993.

Society for Scholarly Publishing. "Publishing and Society Goals." Concurrent Session I, 14th Annual Meeting. Chicago: Society for Scholarly Publishing (1992).

Stubbs, Kendon. "Trends in University Funding for Research Libraries." *ARL (A Bimonthly Newsletter of Research Library Issues and Actions).* January 1994.

Swan, John. "The Electronic Straightjacket." *Library Journal.* Volume 118, Number 17, October 15, 1993.

Thatcher, Sanford G. Privately circulated letter to Ann Okerson, December 3, 1991.

Triangle Research Libraries Network (Copyright Policy Task Force). "Model University Policy Regarding Faculty Publication in Scientific and Technical Scholarly Journals: A Background Paper and Review of the Issues." July 1993.

Ulrich's International Periodicals Directory 1992-93. 33rd Edition. New Providence, N.J.: R. R. Bowker (1992).

Veliotes, Nicholas A. "Publishers and Libraries: More Alike than Different," *Against the Grain,* September, 1993.

Wedgeworth, Robert. "Remaking Scholarly Publishing." *The Chronicle of Higher Education.* Volume 40, Number 17, December 15, 1993.

Williams, Jeffrey. "Academic Libraries: 1990" E. D. TABS, National Center for Education Statistics, U. S. Department of Education, Office of Educational Research and Improvement (1992).

Yavarkovsky, Jerome. "A University-Based Electronic Publishing Network," *EDUCOM Review*, Vol. 25, No. 4, 1990.

ORDER FORM

Council on Library Resources/Association of American Publishers, Inc

LIBRARIANS AND PUBLISHERS IN THE SCHOLARLY INFORMATION PROCESS:
Transition in the Electronic Age

A report from the Joint Working Group
on Professional and Scholarly Information in the Electronic Age
under the sponsorship of the Council on Library Resources
and the Professional/Scholarly Publishing Division, Association of American
Publishers, Inc.

(ISBN: 0-933636-30-X)

Return to:
Association of American Publishers/PSP Division
71 Fifth Avenue
New York, NY 10003-3004
FAX: 212-255-7007
PHONE: 212-255-0200 x 224

Quantity: *Total:*

_____   @ $25.00 $_____

Ship to:
Name_____
Title_____
Company_____
City_____State_____Zip_____

Prices include shipping & handling within the U.S. and Canada. For shipments
outside the U.S. and Canada, **please add $2.00** per copy shipping charge.

Payment enclosed:

_____*Check (made payable to AAP/PSP Division)*

_____*Credit Card:* _____*VISA* _____*Master Card* _____*American Express*

*Credit Card #*_____*Expiration Date: Month*_____*Year*_____

*Signature: (As it appears on credit card):*_____